W9-CDK-920

The
MICROSOFT
EDGE

ALSO BY JULIE BICK

All I Really Need to Know in Business I Learned at Microsoft

Published by POCKET BOOKS

The
MICROSOFT
EDGE

INSIDER STRATEGIES
FOR BUILDING SUCCESS

JULIE BICK

POCKET BOOKS
New York   London   Toronto   Sydney   Singapore

POCKET BOOKS, a division of Simon & Schuster Inc.
1230 Avenue of the Americas, New York, NY 10020

Copyright © 1999 by Julie Bick

All rights reserved, including the right to reproduce
this book or portions thereof in any form whatsoever.
For information address Pocket Books, 1230 Avenue
of the Americas, New York, NY 10020

ISBN: 0-671-03413-8

First Pocket Books hardcover printing November 1999

10 9 8 7 6 5 4 3 2 1

POCKET and colophon are registered trademarks of
Simon & Schuster Inc.

Printed in the U.S.A.

*For my father, who has the greatest instinct
for business I've ever encountered, and for my mother,
whose kindness, enthusiasm, and generosity
make her my role model.*

ACKNOWLEDGMENTS

Thanks first and most to my Microsoft friends and colleagues who shared their war stories, lessons, and time. Without their help, this would have been a really short book. They include Janet Angell, Robbie Bach, Rich Barton, Samir Bodas, Jeff Camp, Brad Chase, Eva Corets, Jon DeVaan, Dean Hachamovitch, Kathleen Schoenfelder Hebert, Michael Hebert, Amy Iorio, Jharna Jain, Mike Kinsley, Yusuf Mehdi, Mike Nash, Lauri Perry, Chris Peters, Paige Prill, Jeff Raikes, Jon Reingold, Jon Roberts, CJ Liu Rosenblatt, Gideon Rosenblatt, Jack Shaeffer, Andrew Short, Ron Sousa, Andrea Tevlin, Dennis Tevlin, Jeff Thiel, Rick Thompson, Hank Vigil, Ben Waldman, Kristin Weeber, Susan Weeber, and Christine Winkel.

Thanks also to my agent, Daniel Greenberg, who always has great ideas and the time to share them, and to Greer Kessel Hendricks, who besides editing the manuscript, tracked and explained a striking array of book-publishing information to me. Most authors probably just write and then leave you alone, huh?

Thank you to Rogers for your encouragement and sense of humor, to Bettijean Collins for your advice and generosity, and to Zelda Madden for keeping the peace downstairs. My gratitude again to those who helped me land in the publishing world, Jon Karp and my uncle, Don Franklin. The executive producer of this book is Mike R. Elliott.

CONTENTS

The
MICROSOFT
EDGE

Introduction

According to a *New York Times* article, "when mothers used to tell their children that they could grow up to be anything they wanted, they usually cited the presidency as the greatest possible aspiration. Now mothers are more likely to tell their kids that they can grow up to be the next Bill Gates." Microsoft has done more to shape the high-technology industry than any other company, and high technology is shaping global society more and more. We've all read about Bill Gates, the boy-wonder Harvard dropout who built the empire, but it takes more than one person to keep a company of thirty thousand employees thriving. More than thriving, actually. The *Wall Street Journal* calls Microsoft "the greatest stock-market success of the century."

How do they do it? The answer combines a relentless focus on achievement with a bit of paranoia and a business culture that pays more attention to breaking convention than operating by it. Let me take you behind the scenes to share some of Microsoft's best practices—practices you can apply to your own job in any line of business.

This book is a follow-up to my first, *All I Really Need to Know in Business I Learned at Microsoft*. The format—short lessons and insider stories—is similar, but *The Microsoft Edge* covers new areas. Whereas the first book focused more on the personal side of business, including how to be a good boss, manage your career, and do your job well, *The Microsoft Edge* focuses on the business side of business: launching new products, doing business on the Web, and working with partners. As with the first book, I'm donating half the proceeds I make from this one to children's charity.

I spent five years at Microsoft as a marketer, new-product planner, and manager. In addition to my own experience, I've drawn on the experiences of forty company managers—including eight vice presidents—for this book to learn even more about *Managerius nerdum competitus* (okay that's not really the Latin name for this species) and how they run their businesses so well. This book isn't an exhaustive encyclopedia of Microsoft processes and procedures. It is a collection of lessons and habits that the managers themselves would say keep Microsoft on top. No, there's not much mention of the Department of Justice lawsuit (too contentious at this writing), and yes, some names and details have been changed to protect the innocent, but reading this book will give you a good idea of what people do day to day at Microsoft, how they make decisions—how they succeed.

Microsoft managers are smart and paranoid. They try to obsolete their own products before someone else does it for them. They're always looking over their shoulder, going as far as inventing "what-if" competitors if the ones around them aren't scary enough. They enter new markets with gusto, whether it's a nascent one on the Web or an established category dominated by big players. For example, Microsoft's version of Barney, the purple dinosaur, was the first toy ever to interact with a TV show and became one of the year's top-selling children's toys, even though the team had scant experience in the toy market.

Microsoft managers have a sense of humor. When a Lotus executive was quoted in a magazine saying that Microsoft manager Dennis Tevlin had the marketing acumen of a toad, Dennis went out and got a nameplate for his door that read OFFICE OF THE TOAD. They also need a pretty thick skin. Imagine presenting to Bill Gates and hearing, "Did you even get to the third minute of thinking about this?!"

Microsoft managers are taught to stay focused, no matter how disruptive outside influences get. In the midst of the

Department of Justice lawsuit, Bill Gates, COO Bob Herbold, and now-president Steve Ballmer told employees to stay focused on building the best products and doing the right thing for customers. Don't let up on the intensity. Let the lawyers worry about the rest, they said in a presentation that was broadcast around the company and into lunchrooms.

But do you need multimillion-dollar marketing programs, thousands of salespeople, R&D scientists with patents, and worldwide subsidiaries to succeed? Surprisingly, no. So try following these admonitions. I can't promise you'll be the next Bill Gates, but I do think your enterprise will thrive, your Web site will generate more traffic, and you'll have better relationships with the people who do business with you.

Let me know how it works out.... E-mail me at JulieW@ MSN.com.

CHAPTER 1

People:
Hiring the Best
and Keeping Them

Great experience? Fabulous references? A winning attitude? Nah! Most Microsoft managers will say "hiring smart people" has been the key to the company's success and will be to its future. As with most disciplines, Microsoft attacks this one with vigor. Employee "success indicators" are compiled, analyzed, and sent around via e-mail. Thousands of employees conduct interviews, and they are trained on what to ask job candidates and how to ask it. Human resource people seek out star performers when they become unhappy and work behind the scenes to get them back in the groove. And despite the fact that they are multimillionaires, hundreds of "old-timers" (well, maybe they're in their mid to late thirties by now) come to work every day. Why do people choose to join at Microsoft and why do they stay?

In a 1998 talk at San Jose State, Bill Gates said, "We like people who have got an enthusiasm for the product, technology, who really believe that it can do amazing things. We're very big on hiring smart people, so you'd better be comfortable ... having the debate and questioning that goes along with that." He's delivered the same sentiment innumerable times, and that opinion has suffused the ranks at Microsoft.

HIRING THE BEST

NEW EMPLOYEE SUCCESS FACTORS

You need to hire someone to fill a spot on your team. Or maybe it's time to go and recruit at the local college. Before you start, sit down with your prospective employee's coworkers and any other folks who will be conducting interviews. Brainstorm and debate the qualities you're looking for to focus everyone on finding the right person for the job. Is it a strategic thinker you're looking for? Are world-class communication skills important? Maybe you're looking for passion and drive. Talk about the kind of person who will excel in the job. Agreeing up front on what's important will have everyone looking for the same qualities in a candidate.

Microsoft focuses on the following "success factors" when hiring employees:

- Individual excellence
- Results
- Teamwork
- Passion for products and technology
- Long-term approach
- Customer focus
- Functional/technical knowledge/skills

Each factor may have subfactors. For example, integrity, intellectual horsepower, composure, and creativity are some of the pieces that make up individual excellence. A team from Human Resources working with managers and executives from around the company crystallized these factors. The weighting might change between jobs or groups—a junior software tester might need to focus on individual excellence and results, while a midlevel marketer might need to have a stronger long-term view of his or her work—but the characteristics fit surprisingly well over the 30,000 employees of the company.

Microsoft holds interviewing workshops to help managers make sure that these factors are evaluated during any employee interview. A list of sample interview questions offers ways to get a candidate to show off these attributes or to demonstrate their absence. There are even tips on finding out if a "success factor" is overdone and possibly detrimental to the candidate's performance. For instance, a person who tells you he'll change any established procedure for any customer request may be taking "customer focus" a bit too far.

Your list of key attributes can be used beyond recruiting. When a new hire joins the team, sit down together and make a list of the skills you both think are important to the success of his or her job and why. Yes, you already have your list in mind. But talking it over together helps both of you focus and is a more palatable approach than a direct order. The discussion sets appropriate expectations for the new employee and can serve as a reminder of the qualities needed to succeed in the position.

Three Lessons I've Learned about Hiring Great Employees

Jon DeVaan, Vice President, Consumer and Commerce Group:

1. **Always hire people smarter than you.**
   Don't be intimidated by them—seek them out!
2. **Take people out of their comfort zone in the interview; make them think.**
   After all, that's what they'll be doing when they get to the job, not reciting memorized answers to standard questions.
3. **After the interview write down in useful detail why you want to hire the candidate or not.**
   "Bong goes the bozo bell" may be fun to say but doesn't give useful information to other interviewers.

HIRE THE PERSON FOR THREE JOBS, NOT ONE

The best hire is a versatile hire. If the market changes, the division is reorganized, or a new business opportunity comes along, you want an office full of people who have the diversity of talents to switch gears to meet the new challenges. If your hire is too specialized, you may find yourself with dead weight and a slot you wish you could fill with different skills.

Sam, an interview candidate in the Human Resources department, had a highly valued talent. Sam could coach anybody through anything. He could help managers work through team-building challenges. He could get the person with "analysis paralysis" to stop overanalyzing data and move forward on a decision. He could help nervous presenters conquer their fear of public speaking. But that's all he could or wanted to do.

There were a number of other responsibilities in the department, but Sam just wanted to stick to his coaching. He didn't want to design programs to take groups of people through a management exercise. He didn't want to research why people were leaving Microsoft and figure out ways to keep them. He didn't want to do team-building exercises. Still, he was hired and excelled as he coached people.

After some time, though, Sam ran out of people to help. Other important issues and projects began looming in the department. Those problems got juggled around the hallway as other team members tried to add them to their own responsibilities. Only Sam stuck to his original charter. But that charter was quite limited. Eventually, Microsoft had to let Sam go and hire someone more flexible.

It's hard to know the "next big thing" that upper management or the market will throw your team. Having a versatile group, supplemented with specifically skilled consultants, when needed, gives you a flexible and cost-effective way to meet new challenges.

RETAINING THE STARS

WHEN MAKING CHANGES,
A LITTLE HUMAN GOES A LONG WAY

You *can* make change easier for your staff. New bosses, new organizations, new responsibilities, can range from somewhat unsettling to downright scary. I had a friend who woke up in a sweat at 2 A.M. every night the week before her first meeting with her new boss. I've seen other teams spend so much time speculating on impending organizational changes that they basically did little work for a month.

Whether it's learning everyone's name and one thing about them ("Hey, Pete, how's your puppy?") or hosting a Friday happy hour in your office, show your employees you're a regular person to allay their misgivings and enable them to be productive quickly in their new roles.

When Brad Chase was the Vice President of Windows Marketing, he was put in charge of combining the Microsoft-DOS and Windows teams. People got nervous. Who would report to whom in this new organization? Where would the power lie? Who would make the big decisions? And who was this guy Brad they'd all be working for now?

Brad sensed the uneasiness in his new group, so he went from office to office meeting with each person on the new team, to discuss their career goals and interests, and to solicit input into the new organization. He told them he would try to match their interests to the business's needs, but that there were no guarantees—mapping out organizations involves chess moves where one decision impacts another. Soon after, Brad called an "all hands" meeting to unveil the new team structure, mission, and top objectives.

As he unveiled the org chart, a chuckle rippled through the audience. The top box—the place of highest rank—contained not the name Bill Gates, but the names of Brad's two toddlers!

Was Bill Gates at least next in line? No, next came Brad's wife, Judy, followed by Brad's administrative assistant. *Then,* Bill appeared along with the other vice presidents and so on down the line.

Brad's org chart showed the team that his priority was his family and gave the message that he understood if the team members weren't at work twenty-four hours a day. Two years later another reorganization was announced, and Brad received some requests to "bring the old org chart" when he met with his teams.

As the group got going, Brad would periodically take mini-polls to get their views on how things were running and would speak to team managers to get input on the biggest areas of opportunity and the biggest roadblocks. Once a quarter, Brad would hold an "all hands" meeting to discuss the results of the polls and the manager feedback, as well as the state of the business. This helped him keep in touch with his teams and let the teams know their opinions were heard and valued.

Three Lessons I Learned about Managing a Group

Dean Hachamovitch, Group Program Manager, Office:

1. **No matter how big the assignment, give it just one owner.**
   If you make the project a group responsibility, each person thinks the others will get it done. One person who knows they're on the line is much more effective.
2. **I tell my team their goal is not to send e-mail or to write a memo but to actually communicate information.**
   The "Rule of Least Surprises" is a good one. No one should say about us, "They did what!"
3. **I try to hire the type of person who asks, "What are the tough issues?" rather than one who asks, "What will Bill Gates say?" (or any other boss).**
   You don't want a team that thinks, "Bill's going to sneeze, so we all need to make tissues!"

Five Ways to Make Sure Your Employees Will Look for Another Job

Microsoft, just like any other company has its share of not-so perfect managers. Rather than "brainstorm," they like to "blamestorm," meeting to discuss why a mistake was made and who did it. Rather than supporting and promoting your work, they're more like pigeons—flying in suddenly, making a lot of noise, and dropping a load all over everything you just did. Here are a few examples to avoid.

AGREE IN PRIVATE, DISAPPEAR IN PUBLIC

"What a wonderful idea," my friend's manager told her. "Why don't you propose it at the next staff meeting?" My friend was excited that her boss liked her work. She was excited to show off her innovative thinking. She was excited to . . . well, you get the idea. At the meeting she breathlessly let everyone in on her new scheme. Her presentation was met with silence—until someone higher up the ladder said, "That's crazy. We'll never make money doing that."

People in the room—those spineless weasels—nodded. After all, her accuser was higher up in the organization and therefore less risky to agree with. She looked at her boss in anticipation. He had liked the idea in his office. Surely, he'd come to her rescue. Instead, she watched as he intently studied a speck on his pen. He didn't look up. She realized she had just been hung out to dry—very publicly.

As a manager, when you tell an employee you support his or her idea, that support should not be conditional based on who is in the room. Standing up for your team engenders respect, trust, and loyalty. They'll feel comfortable bringing you their best propositions and hypotheses.

PUT YOUR NAME ON THEIR WORK

A young woman was asked to write up notes from the day's meeting. She sent them to her boss, who made some incredibly value-added changes, such as switching *households* to *HH* and *Multiple Dwelling Units* to *MDU*. He then E-mailed the notes to his boss with the opening "Here are my key thoughts from the meeting." The young woman caught on quickly and looked for a boss who wasn't afraid to let his hires shine.

A manager who thinks he or she has the right to take credit for an employee's work, just because he or she assigned it or reviewed it, needs to attend remedial social skills training, let alone Management 101 class. Even if you make substantive changes or give crucial advice, give employees credit for the work they did—don't put your name on their results.

GIVE YOUR TEAM PET NAMES

At Microsoft, members of one technical group were *briefly* called Pixel Spice, Web Spice, and Server Spice after the Spice Girls rock group. This is not recommended.

REVIEW BY PAYCHECK

Every six or twelve months, depending on their seniority, Microsoft employees are reviewed by their managers. Based on their job performance, employees might receive a raise, a bonus, or stock options. Unfortunately, some bosses aren't very timely in communicating review scores and raise information to their teams. Since the new pay level appears on the employee's paycheck on a certain date whether or not the boss has actually talked to the employee, these employees end up guessing their review score based on the new dollar amount. This "management by paycheck" has encouraged more than a handful of complaints to the Human Resources Department.

When bosses won't even take fifteen minutes to discuss the things an employee cares about most, his or her job performance and salary level, they send a signal that they don't care about that employee. People need the straight scoop on their performance—good or bad. Sometimes, the best long-run morale boost comes from specific negative feedback that clarifies what someone needs to improve. Timely, clear communication will propel you up the manager popularity rankings—a nice way to get your name known around the water cooler.

STIFLE DISSENT

The top marketer of a business unit at Microsoft mentioned to one of his colleagues a concern he had with the group's strategy. An hour later, the head of the group asked him to come to her office. When he arrived, the leader sat facing him with three of her cronies and said, "We're concerned you won't be effective marketing this product if you don't agree with our strategy."

She didn't want to hear his opinion, debate the product direction, or find out what his concerns were. The project was eventually disbanded—perhaps because his concerns were valid and lay unaddressed. Disgruntled, the marketer decided to leave the group. The situation should have been win-win with problems addressed and a concerned employee listened to. Instead, there were bad feelings all around.

DON'T WAIT UNTIL THEY THREATEN TO LEAVE
(TO FIND OUT WHAT THEY NEED TO STAY)

Respect and appreciate your employees before someone else does. Some managers wait until their employees are so frustrated that they're on the verge of quitting to say, "Oh, great work you're doing." These bosses can't and don't keep talented players on their team.

Frank had been in Microsoft's CD-ROM area in a variety of marketing roles. He had worked with everyone under the sun, from the ad agency to foreign subsidiaries to researchers. He had created scripts to help salespeople show off the best features of a product. He had helped with research to identify consumer-buying habits—for example, owners of Microsoft's Cinemania movie guide were good targets for Microsoft's Encarta encyclopedia. He'd interview kids to see how they liked the new products Microsoft was creating. He had even worked with the international product managers, putting together sales materials for them to translate so they wouldn't each have to reinvent the same work.

To round out his skills, Frank wanted to work with the press; so for months he asked his boss if he could work on the PR. He wanted to show off new products to reporters on press tours. He wanted to be a company spokesperson and felt he was ready to do so.

His boss repeatedly said no. The boss told Frank he wasn't experienced enough in creating marketing messages and that more senior people were in line ahead of him for the job. Fed up, Frank looked around the company and found a PR job in another division. When he told his boss that he was leaving, the PR slot in his group magically opened up just for him!

Frank would have been overjoyed at the offer if his boss had made it earlier. Instead, he felt this was a last-ditch effort to keep him on the team. Yes, that demonstrated he was valuable. But why couldn't he have been shown this before? Now, it was too late. Frank would've preferred to stay. He liked the product and his coworkers. But he no longer trusted his boss. He thought, "Is this someone I have to go to extremes with before I get what I want?" Frank moved on.

The longer you wait to recognize what your employees need to be happy, the more likely it is you'll lose them. Whether it's a change of responsibilities, a promotion, or just ergonomic chairs to soothe their backs, do what your team needs to keep them thriving on the job.

BE AS RELIGIOUS ABOUT RETENTION
AS YOU ARE ABOUT RECRUITING

The old adage "it's cheaper to keep a good customer than to find a new one" makes sense with employees as well. Keeping top performers and experienced managers is usually easier than finding and developing new ones. The departure of intellectual capital—brain drain—coupled with the cost to recruit, hire, and train a replacement makes it just as important to keep your key players happy as it is to do all that college interviewing.

But how many companies have "retention specialists," or official "retention programs"? Compare the hours spent reviewing new résumés, interviewing entry-level candidates, and giving campus presentations, to hours spent making sure key players are motivated, learning, and happy. The former often leaves too little energy for the latter.

After a number of high-level resignations, the executives and the Human Resources Department at Microsoft realized they needed to pay more attention to their most critical employees. And so recently, "on-campus" recruiting has taken on another meaning at Microsoft. A whole panoply of HR specialists use the same lingo of compensation packages, development opportunities, and the like...but they use it in discussions with the people who are already "on (the Microsoft) campus."

WHO'S "LOOSE IN THE SOCKET"?

Managers and HR folks at Microsoft look for warning signs that their key players are "loose in the socket." In other words, a star is at risk to leave the company. They may flag top performers with any of the following behaviors:

- Low engagement in the business or low energy
- A decline in review scores

- Complaints from them to managers or coworkers
- Excessive complaints about them from the team they manage
- Spending more time stabilizing their group than getting anything done
- Stagnation—they have not gotten a promotion in a while (i.e., stuck in a level or job)
- Turmoil—they've been through a few bosses, group reorganizations, or other unsettling changes in the past year

WHICH LEVERS TO PULL
AND WHO SHOULD PULL THEM?

When a top performer gets "loose in the socket," the HR manager, the person's boss, and a mentor or other people close to that employee's career meet to discuss the employee. What data do they have on the employee's performance? Has he or she been through something significant recently? Should the employee be moved or perhaps receive more training in the current job? If they need to be convinced to stay, who can do the convincing? Their boss or someone higher? A mentor? Someone they respect up in the food chain?

In one case, a manager named John in Microsoft's Internet product group told his boss he was being recruited by a local start-up, a hot Seattle company. John's boss, a Human Resources representative, and the vice president of the division met to figure out how to keep John at Microsoft. He was a seven-year Microsoft veteran and had great people skills. Plus, in the past few years, he had gained great Internet business experience that was critical to the company. They knew money wasn't the issue for John. He would almost certainly move to a job with lower compensation if he went to the start-up. They realized that it was the decision-making power in his potential new job—the ability to act more entrepreneurial and not have to get approval from other businesses before moving on a decision—that was enticing him. Knowing this was his hot button, the manager's boss and the VP made a list of changes that they could make and other aspects that, unfortunately, were nonnegotiable. They laid the facts on the table. John agreed to stay if the fixes were made to his job.

In another case, an employee who also happened to be a Rhodes Scholar physicist and sculptor was increasingly dissatisfied with his job. He told his boss he was going to quit to do more sculpting. "What is it about sculpting that you love so much?" his boss asked. The two discussed how the employee missed the experimentation and creation associated with sculpting. The next day, the boss walked into his employee's office and said, "If we change your job to be in charge of prototyping new user scenarios and experimenting with design, would you consider staying?" After some thought the employee agreed. His manager had been able to pinpoint the source of his dissatisfaction—lack of creativity in his work—and revitalized the employee by using this information to change his job.

Three Lessons I've Learned about Coaching Employees

Jeff Raikes, Group Vice President,
Worldwide Sales and Marketing Division

1. **Make "lowlights" a standard part of any business review.**
   People are afraid to give bad news, but that's often the most critical information you need to improve the business. I ask for both highlights and "lowlights" all the time, and the lowlights come first. When employees know it's standard practice to discuss challenges and what can be improved, and that everyone else is doing the same, they're more likely to paint the whole picture.

2. **No matter how small a team or subsidiary is, it's still worth your best effort as a coach.**
   Make sure each management team is strong. Take the time to examine their business challenges and to focus them on a few key strategies. I've seen this really pay off...we expect our Polish subsidiary to sell more than $50 million of software this year.

3. **What to do when you don't want to hire more people but the ones you have think they are overworked?**
   Help them to prioritize their work. Make their goals so unambiguous and focused that they know exactly what to spend time on and what they can drop. Everyone can find wasted efforts in the things they do every day. Help your team streamline their activities so they can make it home for dinner.

TURN EVERYDAY ASSIGNMENTS INTO
EMPLOYEE COMPENSATION

Everyone knows there are different forms of compensation—salary, stock, bonus, vacation, medical benefits. And most people know there are some additional, less obvious forms of compensation, such as an office with a view, a rookie-of-the-year award, a parking spot with your name on it. As a manager, you give assignments and parcel out resources all the time. You can turn these actions into "compensation" if you do it right.

There's a new intern coming and he needs a boss for the summer. You bought five new PCs for your group. Someone needs to go to a trade show in Dallas. Things happen in an office all the time that can be turned into a reward for a job well done.

Summer interns at Microsoft are often assigned to someone who's never been a manager before but is just about ready to become one. Typically, a summer hire needs lots of instruction, direction, and can take up a good deal of a manager's time. If you walk into the office of a manager-in-waiting and say, "You're doing a great job. You're almost ready to be promoted to manager. To help get you there, I'd like you to manage this person for the summer," the manager-in-waiting is now a manager-in-training. He or she is usually overjoyed at the opportunity, and you've found the summer hires a boss eager to spend time with them.

Five new PCs are sitting in boxes, waiting to be distributed to your team. Walk into a junior person's office and say, "You've been working hard on your project and I really appreciate it. We're getting some new computers for the team. Why don't you come down and take first pick." The order and manner in which you divvy up the resources can turn into compensation.

When I worked on the Microsoft Word marketing team (most of whom were in their early to mid twenties), business trips were often assigned by the location of the employee's parents. The native Texan went to customer visits and trade shows in that state. The East Coast transplants made most of their trips to New York, Boston, and D.C. Business travel became free trips home. It couldn't strictly be called compensation, but it was used to boost morale. For other trade shows and business trips, the team's manager often asked for volunteers. Sometimes he'd reward an employee who had volunteered for a grueling trip with business travel to Denver during ski season.

In some cases you may not know what employees would really value as extra compensation. Is it more time off? A quieter office? Getting out of an unpleasant task? Let them take their pick. As manager of a software design team, Dean Hachamovitch likes to give out "Get out of Jail Free" cards when he asks someone to go over and above the regular workload.

Eric LeVine, a member of Dean's technical team, was putting in long nights getting the last kinks out of Word 97 so it would ship on time. In the meantime, the marketing team couldn't get the prerelease version to work, to allow them to write a demonstration script, or "demo," of the product. If the demo didn't get written by the launch, no one would see Word 97 at its best. Eric had both technical expertise and understood customer-usage scenarios.

When Dean asked him to help the marketing team, Eric said, "That's going to hurt."

Dean thought about the standard boss lines he could use on Eric:

- You should do this, it will be good for your career
- This is very important for the company
- You are the only one who can do this right

Rejecting those, Dean replied, "I understand that. How about if I make you a Get out of Jail Free card. You can use it anytime for anything you want." Eric chuckled and agreed.

Dean's employee's have used their Get Out of Jail Free cards for a variety of wishes. In one case, a team member decided to leave Microsoft to become an environmental lawyer. He wrote a note, "Dean, I'd like you to write my law school recommendation," and included the Get out of Jail Free card.

SETTLERS VS. PIONEERS

Rick Thompson, the vice president in charge of Microsoft's hardware division, is known for saying that it takes "settlers" and "pioneers" to run a great business. The pioneers spearhead new products and take big risks. They fail with flourish as loudly as when they succeed brilliantly. The settlers, in contrast, keep the established businesses running smoothly. They are deliberate, purposeful, patient, and rigorous in their attention to detail. They'll use innovation to improve the business too, but not as radically as the pioneers. Both types are critical to the health of an organization.

Identify the pioneers and settlers on your team and assign them to the appropriate projects. Don't go against their natural grain. Promoting a brilliant big-idea-generator to a position responsible for eeking out incremental gains in an established business is most likely the wrong move. Putting a manager who is devoted to the details of administrative procedure on a brainstorming team probably won't yield the best results. Let each type of person use his or her strengths to get great work done.

As Rick says, "Pioneers can't settle down, and settlers would die out in the wilderness. But, together they can do amazing things."

LET THE PIONEERS GO A LITTLE WILD

At Microsoft, products are normally "spec'd out" (i.e., the product's specifications are planned down to the minutiae) before they are built. Details on customer needs, features, and the look of the product are all carefully laid out and scheduled. Pioneers, however, want to show up and immediately start building prototypes. They're passionate about an idea and want to jump on it. Let them. Don't force pioneers to abide by company policy, dotting every I and crossing each T. Let the skunk works flourish—although as a manager you'll be "worried the whole time," Rick warns. Will cost objectives be met? Will the project get done on time? Will the thing even work? Try to relax. Microsoft gives pioneers the time and money to investigate their inspiration.

In 1998, a Microsoft pioneer had a great idea for a children's product. It combined the idea of a pager, a Nintendo Game Boy, and a walkie-talkie. This small device would allow children to send and receive typed messages transmitted by radio wave. A tiny camera could transmit pictures as well. Everything on the project was put into children's terms. For example, the operating radius of the device was measured at two to three classrooms wide, as opposed to a number of feet.

After months of research, the team concluded that while the product was cool, there was no lasting competitive advantage for Microsoft. Nintendo could easily come in and do the team one better, using its existing game-boy device and adding the new functionality. Nintendo already had the scale in place to undercut Microsoft's costs and the game cartridges to deliver extra revenue. The division managers were disappointed that the product wouldn't work for Microsoft, but no one regretted the time or money spent to come to this conclusion. Good pioneers know when to turn back.

In another case, a Microsoft pioneer found inspiration in a medical-instrument simulator that helped surgeons feel what it would be like to operate on someone. As a person moved the medical-simulation instrument, they'd feel the push back as if they were cutting through human tissue. Gross as this sounds, it inspired the Microsoftie to create a joystick for PC games. The "force feedback" joystick let gamers feel the speedup of a plane or the g-force of a turn. With little planning and an extremely tight time frame, the Microsoft joystick was created and launched. In just the first ninety days it sold 225,000 units at $149 each, a huge accomplishment. The quality of the product was a success too—the U.S. space agency, NASA, even requested some joysticks from Microsoft.

SETTLERS NEED TO INNOVATE WITHOUT PUTTING
THE BUSINESS IN JEOPARDY

Microsoft sells 25 million mice a year. If the people on that team can make the business 5 percent better, they've just delivered a major boost. Accordingly, the mouse managers look into decreasing component and delivery costs, addressing new sales opportunities at retail and with PC makers. They also try to strengthen intellectual property rights, filing patents so competitors can't copy their work. They are true settlers.

Sometimes though, the settlers on the Microsoft mouse team have a bit of the pioneer itch and come up with an idea that would significantly change an aspect of the business. When an idea like this is proposed, Rick Thompson doesn't bet the whole mouse franchise on it. Instead, the settler team will implement and bulletproof the innovation on the side. The group tests the idea, analyzes it, brutalizes it, builds it, and proves it. But by doing all this in parallel to the main work of the mouse team, they don't risk the entire business.

In 1996, the mouse team felt their "switch" component (basically the little thing under the mouse button that clicks when you press the button down) was priced too high and wanted to build a replacement themselves. Two huge global companies, Matsushita and Omron, were the only suppliers of this part, so there weren't any cheaper alternatives to be found in the market. Making their own switch seemed the best option to the mouse team. They wrote the specifications for a new switch, built it, tested it, investigated the manufacturing of it. Everything looked great. More testing was required, but the outcome seemed promising.

Instead of canceling its switch orders with Matsushita and Omron, and making plans to build and ship its own, Microsoft continued to test. If the switches were as good as they looked, the testing would delay their migration into the product for a while and delay the cost savings; but, if the switches failed, Microsoft would be happy it hadn't changed its entire mouse manufacturing process to accommodate the new component. As work on the project continued, testing showed the new switch was not reliable enough. The effort was abandoned. Because the work was done in parallel to the main business, that main revenue stream was not adversely affected.

AT SOME POINT, A PIONEERING PROJECT TURNS INTO A SETTLER BUSINESS

History shows that the leader of the revolution might not make the best day-to-day president. The inventor might not make the best CEO. The same holds true for the new product created by the pioneer. Once it is well established, the risk-taking, no-schedule, seat-of-the-pants way of managing a product or service needs to give way to a more predictable and stable delivery model for customers. The focus needs to be on faultless execution, rather than innovative breakthroughs.

After its success with the force-feedback joystick, a group of pioneers tried to use the same technology to make a force-feedback steering wheel. They envisioned another great device that would let players of driving-simulation games feel bumps in the road and the power of a hairpin turn. To do this, the team assumed they could reuse the motors used in the force-feedback joystick.

Microsoft went off to a trade show, proudly displaying ten new steering wheels for people to try. Soon, eight of the steering wheels were broken. Because people were using two hands on the wheel, gripping, pulling, turning, versus one hand on the joystick, the device was under much more stress and malfunctioned. In this case, the breakneck schedule of a pioneering team allowed a bad assumption to sneak through. Settlers would have taken more time to test the product.

The bigger problem now was that the first batch of steering wheels were being made at the factory. The hardware team had to stop the production and fix and retest the steering wheels.

To make matters worse, Microsoft had promised the product to retailers by a certain day. Those retailers had paid for ads and had started their promotion efforts. Microsoft had to deliver the steering wheels on time or its mistake would cost those stores a lot of money.

"We had to airfreight *fifty thousand* steering wheels at twenty-seven dollars each," remembers Rick Thompson, the amount etched in his brain. But he admits that the project, if run by true settlers, might have taken so long they would have missed the Christmas selling season. Most projects probably do best with a bit of each—the tough part is finding the right balance of inspiration and execution.

COMPETITORS CAN TEACH YOU INTERESTING THINGS, AND NOT JUST ABOUT PRODUCTS

Don't just analyze a competitor's product line, ad campaign, or technology. Check out their management practices, training programs, compensation packages, and organizational structure. Human resource consortiums and conventions are a great place to learn how to run a more successful business. There is a lot of information other companies can't tell you, but there's a surprising amount they do.

Along with the meetings mentioned above, your company can sponsor research with other companies to benefit the whole group. Microsoft, along with other companies, commissioned a study comparing the companies' management-development, training, and retention practices. From the resulting report, Microsoft made some changes and additions to its existing management and career track practices. Here are a few examples.

MAKE YOUR OWN MAP OF THE STARS

A great tool Microsoft has adopted involves drawing extremely detailed organizational charts of the company. A group of HR folks plot the whereabouts of star performers across all divisions of the company. From that "star map," upper management can see if there is too much talent stacked up in one division, while other important areas need more brainpower.

In other cases, the star map could point out star players who are "trapped" by layers of mediocre management. In one case, a talented woman buried in a subsidiary was pulled out and given a job in another subsidiary. She quickly excelled, just as management had expected. She became a vice president and continued her rise. Another star on the map was exhibiting great leadership potential but his team was so big, his boss didn't have time to help him exercise that talent. He was moved to a group where he could lead a small team himself and develop that skill.

The star map also shows where stars are needed. One lively employee did a great job organizing teams and getting them working at full speed. Management used the star map to identify teams who could use this expertise and then moved the star from group to group like Johnny Appleseed, so he could get each one up and rolling. He'd teach his management technique to the level below him so they could take over when he moved on. The star map showed the Human Resources team where he needed to be placed next.

EMPLOYEE SURVEYS

Like many companies, Microsoft's HR department conducts a yearly survey asking employees about their attitudes toward their job, their boss, and the company. From this, policy changes are made, foundering managers helped, and areas of potential employee unrest recognized.

The survey covers a spectrum of topics, and each can point out a problem that needs fixing. The survey asks employees if they have clear goals, feel challenged, and receive timely feedback from their boss. Spotty answers here may send up a red flag that a certain manager needs help leading his or her team. The survey asks employees if they know what their department's mission is, how it relates to other groups, and if there are barriers to working with those other groups. Confusion here could indicate the need for a reorganization. The survey inquires about employees' trust of the senior executives. Do they believe in the company vision? Do they believe the senior executives are taking the company in the right direction? Do they think Microsoft is missing the boat somewhere?

Overall satisfaction is examined too. There are questions on compensation and work-life balance. Employees are asked how many years they are likely to stay with the company. All the survey data is sliced and diced. Are women more likely to leave the company than men? Do junior people understand the company mission? By asking employees once a year to rate jobs, bosses, other groups, and their own happiness, Microsoft can identify and take action on a wide range of issues.

JUNIOR BOARDROOM: TRAINING THE NEXT LEVEL

Another management-development technique that Microsoft and many other companies use is to give a group of young executives the same set of problems and challenges to mull over as their senior counterparts. For example, Microsoft holds management retreats to think over, investigate, and debate issues such as the future convergence of the Internet and television or how to keep costs down as a percentage of revenue. The junior group is given time to meet and discuss the topics and then give a formal presentation to the senior group or send recommendations via memo or E-mail.

This technique trains the "executives-in-waiting" to think about broad issues that affect the whole company. It gets them used to working on strategy with peers from other areas and lets them show their talent off with (they hope) creative solutions and crisp analysis.

Three Lessons I've Learned about Changing Jobs

Christine Winkel, Product Manager, Microsoft Barney, Teletubbies, and other ActiMates:

1. **Know your boss's place in the company pecking order.**
   Before taking a new job, see how your potential boss is viewed and respected by upper management. What are your boss's overall responsibilities? What types of decisions does he/she own? The most useless person to work for is a manager who isn't respected and doesn't have authority in the organization.

2. **Know your boss's quirks.**
   Everyone has them. Usually, you're better off knowing which ones your boss has before you accept a job working for him/her. Speak to other folks who have worked for him/her in the past. What do they like about the manager? What did they hate? Step back and ask yourself if the boss's style, attitude, and demeanor add up to someone you can flourish under.

3. **Know your boss's skill set.**
   It's vital to find a manager with different skills from yours. The boss will have an easier time letting some control go since you bring something else to the task. A variety of talents within a team are also important from a company's point of view. Managers who pass on new knowledge and experience enhance the skills of their team and prep them for future growth/promotion.

SETTING UP THE SALES FORCE
TO SUCCEED

Holistic probably isn't the word that comes to mind when the Microsoft sales force is mentioned. So it's surprising to see how the sales organization, its initiatives, strategies, measurements, and reviews do actually fit that description, emphasizing the importance of the whole and the interdependence of its parts. As head of that sales and support organization, Jeff Raikes has built a framework to segment customers, find their leverage points, amass a mind-boggling amount of detail on the market, and then act on it, worldwide. The process can get exceedingly complex, but everything is tied back to customers, sales goals, and a few global initiatives.

ORGANIZING EVERYTHING AROUND CUSTOMERS

Because Microsoft sells software, Jeff Raikes, head of the Worldwide Sales and Marketing Division, views the market accordingly, by the number of PCs an organization has. Other businesses, of course, view markets based on what matters most to them. For Microsoft, the biggest segments are

- Large businesses with more than a thousand PCs
- Medium-sized companies with fifty to a thousand PCs
- Small organizations with less than fifty PCs

The Microsoft sales organization encompasses subsidiaries around the world and thousands of sales and support staff. Every aspect of this enormous group is built around "customer units," focused on a segment. At headquarters in Redmond, "customer unit" staffers create sales tools, pricing models, and support materials for their specific segment. In the field offices around the United States, salespeople are divvied up the same way and call only on accounts in their segment. The subsidiaries do the same.

DATA ANALYSIS: EXAMINING THE MARKET, SETTING GOALS

Microsoft collects huge amounts of data on each customer segment, as well as the overall market, competitors, and sales channels. First there's the usual data you might guess a software company tracks:

- How much and what kind of Microsoft software is sold in each country
- How much software the competition sells

Then it gets a little more detailed, including:

- How often PCs are replaced (swapping old ones for new)
- Top companies selling the software to this group
- How much Microsoft makes on each PC for the whole segment

Then it gets downright incredible, such as:

- The amount of revenue the third-largest U.S. reseller derived from selling Oracle databases that run on Microsoft NT software
- Information on 213,000 "value-added providers" in the United States that provide software services to small businesses. Data includes if they've been to a Microsoft seminar and how many E-mails have been sent to them.

The sales management team slices and dices the data every way possible, comparing countries, products—you name it. A hundred-page resulting "yellow book" includes thousands of tiny numbers showing every permutation and combination of the data. The managers use this data to:

1. Know country by country, region by region, segment by segment, where sales are coming from. They can then identify new market opportunities to capitalize upon, and trouble spots that may need some shoring up.
2. Determine who the key players are in the channel and make sure their relationships and programs for them are stellar.
3. Figure out the number and makeup of their customer base. What do those customers look like? What are they buying?
4. Keep track of competitor pricing, sales figures, and marketing spending.
5. Identify anomalies in the data and delve into their causes. Why have sales suddenly stalled in a certain region?
6. Share best practices. Why is SQL Server selling so well in Taiwan? What is the team in that country doing and how can we learn from them?

This level of detail may seem like overkill, but when Microsoft president Steve Ballmer asked if the software sales in the western region of the United States matched population density in that area of the country, a sales manager quickly gave him the answer without referring to any notes.

CREATING GLOBAL INITIATIVES THAT EVERYONE OWNS

Each year, the top sales and support leaders in Jeff's organization use the excruciatingly detailed data of the yellow book and talk with the Microsoft groups creating the next generation of products, to determine five to seven initiatives for the sales force worldwide over the next year. These are separate from sales goals. Initiatives might focus on customers, competitors, partners, or even a new iternal information system to help the sales force become more efficient. Recent initiatives have included lowering the total cost of a PC for a corporation (i.e., software training, installation, and maintenance) and "delighting customers."

The five to seven global initiatives are then given to a task force made up of regional representatives from around the world, and from each customer unit. The makeup of the group reflects the organization, i.e., the customer units, and so it represents the market. This group makes the initiatives actionable by putting guidelines and measurements around them. They answer the questions: "What will success look like for this initiative? How will we know we've done it?" "Do we need to hit a sales target?" "Should we give seminars to a certain number of customers?" By involving representatives from around the world and from different customer units, each group in Jeff's organization feels partly responsible for the resulting goals.

Soon after the initiative group maps out goals and measurements, one thousand Microsoft sales and marketing people from around the world descend on a city to get trained, excited, and prepared to launch those initiatives in their countries. Again, this "global summit" ties back to the customer units, offering information for salespeople calling on each type of customer.

SETTING UP COMPENSATION
TO MEET CORPORATE GOALS

The field's compensation is also tied back to the customer segments and initiatives. There is the usual set of incentives for selling certain products, based on the makeup and needs of the customer segment. There are additional bonuses for making progress on company-wide initiatives such as increasing customer satisfaction or establishing more frequent communication with the retail channel.

There should be no question in the minds of the sales managers exactly how they will be judged. Jeff Raikes sends out a sample presentation they use to create their annual business review. Accompanying the sample presentation is an actual video of Jeff explaining what he expects out of each portion, what he's going to look for, and what he thinks is important. The sample and video probably prepare, excite, and terrify the managers putting the data together. Doubtless, though, they have the desired effect: when sales managers know they're going to be graded on both sales and their progress on the company-wide initiatives, they focus the sales teams on both activities.

Jeff Raikes and his team developed a global market taxonomy and transformed Microsoft's sales and support organization to match it. Jeff makes sure that the organization is supplied with every piece of data it needs to set goals, share best practices, and make decisions. Tying the compensation back to the initiatives and customers completes the circle.

Three Lessons I've Learned about Getting the Best from Your Sales Force

Jeff Raikes, Group Vice President,
Worldwide Sales and Support

1. **Opportunities are everywhere.**

   Keep an eye on the whole market, even at the national policy level. To boost the use of PCs in Japanese businesses, the Japanese government decided to make PCs a business expense with a one-year, rather than a six-year, depreciation write-off. When Japanese companies start buying more computers, that's an opening for us to sell more software, so we really geared up for it.

2. **Look at the real expense of hiring additional people.**

   Calculate three or four years out, taking into account cost increases due to annual raises, health insurance, etc. Does it still make sense for the business for you to hire more employees?

3. **Equip the sales force quickly when a competitor makes a move.**

   When one of our rivals introduces a new product, drops a price, or changes licensing agreements, I like our folks in the field to receive a concise report within two days from headquarters explaining what the move means to customers and how to respond.

CHAPTER 2

Doing Business on the Web

On the Web, the first to learn is the first to win.
— Dennis Tevlin, Former Director of Marketing,
Interactive Media Division

A geneticist at his desk in Sweden reviews a map of the human genome stored in a computer in Germany. A time-crunched mom sees an infomercial and goes to the proffered Web site to order the exercise video. A college student sends his dad an E-mail and then stays at his PC to check out the local bands playing that weekend. It's the new "Web lifestyle," and everybody's joining in.

After a much-publicized late start, Microsoft too has embraced the Web. The company is experimenting with posting information, selling products, offering interactive games, creating ads, and programming TV-like "shows." Microsoft has tested yellow pages, home buying, travel planning, banking alliances, and magazine publishing. It's built subscriber sites, free sites, search engines, and design-your-own news pages. In a very few years, the company has looked into just about everything there is to do on the Web that isn't X-rated.

From their successes and failures, Microsoft managers have learned how to build and nurture communities on the internet. They've become better Web site managers using customer feedback, incremental improvements, and better designs. The home runs and the strikeouts have been equally spectacular, but in most cases, the lessons are surprisingly consistent.

Three Things I Learned about Deciding to Create a Web Site

Hank Vigil, Vice President of
Consumer Strategy and Partnership:

One day, having a Web site may be considered a necessary cost of doing business, the way a yellow-pages listing is today. But right now it's still a luxury, so before you start on your home page, answer a few key questions.

1. **What do want the site to do? What problem will it solve or benefit will it offer?**
You may want to use the site as a marketing tool. Perhaps it'll save money by distributing information or services more cheaply. You may want your Web site to help "care" for customers. Customer service alone has myriad implementations, from directions on how to get to your office building to checking order status.

2. **Do you have the resources to create a truly compelling Web site?**
Your product, your ads, even the voice of the employee who answers your phone, can all leave a positive or negative impression of your company. The Internet does the same thing. A semi-useful, mediocre Web site may do more harm than good.

3. **Will it amplify your business?**
Will the site really move your enterprise forward, or will it cost more than it's worth? A ski resort in Utah can use the Web to attract an international clientele, just by offering information and showing up on the right search-engine results. The local environmental testing business that only sends trucks out in a hundred-mile radius may have less to gain.

DON'T ABANDON YOUR WEB SITE WHEN IT IS "COMPLETE"

Many companies make the mistake of creating a Web site and then letting it stagnate. They decide they need a Web site because everyone else has one. They figure that making information available on-line is a good idea, so they do it and think they're done. But changing technology, increasing traffic on the Web, and growing customer expectations make a static Web site worse than no site at all. Don't budget a decline in your Web-site headcount after you create your site. You may need different skills and talents, but you won't need any fewer of them.

Your Web site is like any other project—there will always be "fixes" to make and little things to improve. Internet technology changes often, more people are on the Web every day, and your competitor is probably building a Web site too.

You have to have a team that can keep up. For example, a new compression system may be available to speed up the performance of your site. With so many Internet surfers abandoning Web sites because they don't have time to wait, adopting the technology could make a big difference in your success. Lots of issues must be kept in mind while you plan the "maintenance" of your Web site.

Competitors and users can spur the need for change too. Perhaps your competitor has added something fabulous to its Web site and you want to match it. Or a customer may have a suggestion that improves your on-line ordering system and you know you just have to implement it. You need a team at the ready to make these changes. If you're lucky, the major reason you'll need to keep updating your Web site is the sheer volume of users. Your Web site needs the capacity to handle the ever-increasing loads.

Not only is it a bad idea to stop improving your Web site, but sometimes you can't even take a break. The employees of Microsoft's Internet magazine, *Slate,* had scheduled a week to go on vacation and not publish. The first day of that week, Britain's Princess Diana was killed in a car crash. People worldwide were turning to the Internet for information, including the readers of *Slate.* Instead of up-to-the-minute news, they found the team was gone! In retrospect, editor Mike Kinsley advises, "Send each half of the team on vacation separately and keep the rest at work in case anything big happens!"

Leave some buffer in the schedule as you create your Web site. Keep your team open to serendipity. If you establish too many requirements, you'll box yourself in. When Mike Kinsley first established *Slate,* he set up a few key areas the magazine would cover. Since then, his team has tried out a variety of additional subject matters, formats, and delivery systems for the webzine's content. If he had planned every feature, hired every writer, and mapped out every detail for the magazine's first six months, he couldn't have responded to reader feedback, news trends, and brainstorms from his staff. The Web is "terra incognita," according to Mike, so latitude and resources for experimentation are required.

Even when you've posted the latest news or information, your Web site isn't "done." According to Mike, readers need "compensation" for reading on-line, rather than from the printed page, where they typically feel more comfortable. So when *Slate* posts information, the team offers additional services only available via the magic of the Web. *Slate*'s "Today's Papers" delivers readers the headlines and analysis of five major newspapers, bright and early each morning. *Slate* "Dispatches" from major events, such as the U.S. senate hearings on campaign finance reform, appear minutes after the events conclude. A good Web site reflects the world, constantly changing with new technology and ideas. Keep your mind open and your staff ready for both.

MAKE IT STICKY

Microsoft tries to make its Web sites "sticky," i.e., yes, they want customers to stick to the Web site. A sticky Web site is one that users prefer over competing Web sites. A sticky Web site also makes a user want to come back more often. More visits translate to more Web pages viewed, which translates to more advertising space to sell and hence more revenue. But making the site sticky means different things to different sites—in some cases, opposite things.

In the early days of the CarPoint Web site, the site's team added new information to their Web pages every day to keep the site "fresh." They imagined people coming there every day or every week, just to see what was going on. The team posted articles on "how air conditioners work in your car" or the latest information on crash-test-dummy design. As usual with the Web, the "hits" told the story. Few users clicked on the daily articles and few came day after day to see what was new. The users of that Web site were going there for one reason: to research and possibly buy a car. They would visit the site for that purpose and then stop. They had little interest in the site's being "fresh." They just wanted it to be current (prices, models, options) and useful and easy. In fact, the "freshness" was just cluttering up the page and getting in the way of researching and buying the cars! From this discovery, the articles on the CarPoint site, especially the rotating new ones, were scaled way back.

The Internet magazine *Slate* found almost the opposite to be true. Mike Kinsley, *Slate*'s editor, started by publishing the magazine once a week. Quickly he realized that people wanted, and that the Internet allowed, a much speedier delivery of news. He started posting a scheduled portion of the magazine each day. Users responded positively and asked for even more frequency and currency. They wanted reporting on the news as it happened. *Slate* postings now come at all hours of the day and night depending on the news. Mike jokes that people now send E-mails like, "Hey, this thing happened 45 minutes ago. Where's your analysis?" For CarPoint users, constant new information didn't make the site sticky. For *Slate*, the more frequent the postings, the stickier the site.

CarPoint has found its own way to get sticky. Users were coming to the site only to research and buy a car, maybe once every few years. The team added a feature that allows users to enter the make and model of their car. Armed with this information, CarPoint is able to notify them of any recalls, maintenance (time to change the oil, rotate the tires), or other information pertinent to their car. This increases the frequency of contact between users and CarPoint.

Every site has its own sticky features. Microsoft Investor, the personal-investing Web site, tracks the performance of stocks specified by a user. And if users indicate a stock and a certain price, Investor will notify them when the stock hits that number. Expedia's fare tracker lets users input a favorite destination and notifies them when special fares come up. By hooking users on your site or getting them to visit more often or giving you an excuse to contact them, sticky Web sites translate to more revenue.

WALK THROUGH YOUR WEB SITE

If you've been to a Toys "Я" Us store lately, you know that you have to walk through oodles of fun toys—which you don't need—to get to the essentials, such as diapers, formula, and baby food, which are stocked at the back of the store. This strategy is great if you want to make sure your customers make an impulse purchase on their way to buying what they really came for. Toys targeting the same age group and gender are grouped together to make shopping easier and to help sell new toys by placing them near the tried-and-true favorites.

Think of your Web site as a retail store, whether you are selling products, services, or just offering information. Guide your on-line customer the same way you would guide someone who just walked into your physical store. Consciously create pathways by thinking about what your visitors need or what you want them to experience, buy, or do. Block pathways that don't make sense. Your Web site design allows more control than a store does, so take advantage of it. And make sure visitors can either contact you or purchase your product from any screen in your Web site.

When he helped create the Microsoft CarPoint Web site, manager Gideon Rosenblatt started by building a site with "lots of information about cars." There was literally something for everyone. Customers could bounce around the site from place to place, depending on their interests. Two years later, the Web site was radically different. It now had a targeted and specifically designed set of paths with limited choices. Gideon and his team based their changes on research that allowed him to see how a customer actually used the site. Taking away paths and choices didn't reduce customer satisfaction—as you might think. Quite the opposite, the changes enhanced the experience and attracted new customers.

Gideon's exercise to create the best pathways in his Web site went something like this:

- Segment the Web site's target market.
- Determine each segment's objectives at the site.
- Design a path that accomplishes the objective of each segment.
- Examine each "page" of each path. He asked, "What should each page accomplish? Are the choices on each page visible and easy to understand?"
- Measure and test the paths with actual traffic.
- Refine and repeat!

Gideon looked first at his target audience. Whom was he attracting to the site? Why were they coming to CarPoint? Whom else did he want to visit? He grouped people into three segments.

The first group were people at the beginning of buying a car. In fact, they had no idea what kind of car they might want. Their objective was simply to gather information. To actually sell a car to someone from this group was a long process. The customer needed to be moved all the way from information gathering, to choosing a car, to pricing the options, to comparing dealer prices and availability, and *then* to buying it.

Gideon chose not to push this group into a quick sale, which would surely have annoyed them anyway. Instead, he included plenty of information they'd find fascinating and relevant. As these customers made their way through CarPoint, they saw manufacturer safety records and lists of awards. Interactive features then helped them narrow their choices based on their lifestyle (how many people would ride in the car, price range, etc.). The option to actually buy a car came far, far down the path. Gideon knew that these customers rarely in one visit went all the way to buying a car. So he wanted to make sure that this group—when they did decide to buy—would remember that CarPoint contained complete and credible information and come back to the site to make a purchase.

The second segment of visitors to the site knew the kind of car they wanted, but needed more information on the model's option prices, resale value, gas mileage, etc. Gideon and his team made sure these pieces of information were easy to find and compare. Since this group of users was closer to purchasing a car, the option to buy one came sooner and in a more obvious way than in the path of the first group. As expected, more from this group did buy a car.

The final segment was the most sophisticated. People here knew the car they wanted. They knew how buying on the Web worked. All they wanted was the best price quote from the CarPoint dealer network. They wanted to go directly to the last step—buying a car. In this case, Gideon made a direct link for them to get a price quote.

For the users, the three paths were clearly visible from the home page, so they could select based on their interest. For the Web design team, every single page of each path had an objective, such as:

- Give information.
- Get information (for example, the address of customers, things they wanted in a car, and even a survey about the site itself).
- Allay privacy fears (explaining security measures).
- Get users hooked (fun activities or ones that took time and commitment).

Each page had a clear answer to the question "What should a user do here?" For example, on a page where Gideon wanted users to "get hooked" on the buying process, his team allowed them to choose the color of their car. Gideon tried to re-create on his Web site the excitement a customer could feel at a real car showroom. He wanted the customer to exclaim, "Great! It comes in midnight blue!" Or have the customer get absorbed in figuring out if the tan leather seats looked better than the black ones in that hot, new Lexus coupe.

His team tested the pathways for his three segments, measuring how many people clicked through the different areas on the Web site. From that data, as well as user surveys, they further refined the pathways and pages. They'd count how many people completed the interactive feature querying them on the type of car they wanted. When too many people dropped out in the middle, they figured it was too long, not useful, or too confusing. When they saw that people balked at providing personal information such as their address, they displayed the privacy and security information first to reassure them it was safe to do so. The research method was a bit like following people around in a store and observing their shopping habits. It was labor-intensive, but Gideon's conscious design and continual refinement of the Web site helped make CarPoint a significantly improved experience for customers and more lucrative for Microsoft.

Three Lessons I Learned about Delighting Customers on the Web

Ben Waldman, General Manager,
Macintosh Business Unit, and creator of the
Mactopia Web site:

1. **Use every aspect of the site to make your audience feel at home.**
   We used the retro fonts and colors of the new iMac machines for our Web site. The Microsoft corporate folks hated the idea, but the Mac customers said, "Wow, it's really a Mac Web site!"

2. **You can never go wrong with free stuff.**
   We started our Web site with a contest to win a new iMac machine—that was a big hit. Now we give away lesson plans for teachers and K–12 interactive tutorials, business templates, help files, product add-ons, and are always looking for more things our customers might like.

3. **Go beyond the above and beyond.**
   Macintosh customers expected to find only dry product information on our Web site. We surprised them by adding links to news about Apple, the Macintosh community, and access to the product development team. The free stuff and the Apple iMac colors and fonts also pleased them.

GET IN FRONT OF A BAD EXPERIENCE

The news of a customer's bad experience spreads like wild-
fire on the Internet. Screw up someone's order, put them on an
electronic mailing list they don't want to be on, or post some
incorrect information, and you may find yourself being electronically skewered. With a few mouse clicks, your customers
can E-mail their friends, flood you with complaints, and post
their displeasure on public bulletin boards read by thousands
of people...maybe even on your own Web site!

There are bound to be miscalculations and lost data—some
minor and some severe—as a Web site gets up and running. By
monitoring performance, accepting blame, and quickly fixing
problems, you may be able to stay ahead of an irate Internet
user's mayhem.

One day, the Expedia travel team received this E-mail message, "I ordered a $600 ticket through Expedia—and when it
came in the mail, Expedia had charged $1,100 to my credit
card!"

A collective groan went up through the people working on
the site. They quickly looked into the problem and found that
1 percent of all tickets were mispriced. Now, if 99 percent of
all McDonald's hamburgers came the way they were ordered
and 1 percent were not, that would be okay. A few people
might be one pickle short, but no big deal. If 99 percent of all
flights in the United States landed at the correct airport and 1
percent didn't, that would be just plain unacceptable. Now
ticket mispricing may not be quite that extreme, but it is still
enough to make a customer angry, especially when the mistake
amounts to several hundred dollars.

The team determined they'd have to close down the Web
site to fix the snafu. They posted a message that said, "We're
fixing a problem, please call if urgent!" They had no choice but

to take the site down for eighteen hours, which was akin to closing the cash register and losing sales.

To minimize the damage to customers, the Expedia team tracked down the affected users via E-mail, notified them of the discrepancy, and reimbursed them the difference. The team also apologized profusely and sent gifts (in this case Microsoft Office software!)

Next, to minimize the fallout, they went to the message boards on their site and indeed found some "flame mail" posted there. This is equivalent to customers of a store writing hate mail and posting it inside the store for other customers to see. The Expedia team posted notices that they were aware of the problem, were fixing it, and were reimbursing those affected. They likened that to posting a bigger I'M SORRY sign on the front door of their store. "We knew we had to move fast," said Rich Barton, the Expedia general manager. "When you run an Internet site, everything happens at rocket speed. Embrace that speed and use it or you'll get burned by it."

CONSTANT PRODUCT IMPROVEMENTS

In the "real" world, you may have no idea how customers are using your product. Does the person who bought your exercise video use it once a week with friends, three times a week at 6 A.M., or never, because they hate it?

Of course you can make better decisions when you know how the product is used. But how can you obtain that data? Microsoft would actually ask to follow people home (yes, they went to the customer's house) to watch how they used software. In contrast, the Web can almost automatically show you who is using what and how by counting "hits." A hit is counted when a person clicks on a certain page or image on the Web site.

Combine this with your ability to make immediate updates to your Web site, and you have a powerful dynamic. In the "real" world, you send a product to market and can't make any changes. The package is on the shelf or the brochure is on the counter and there's no fiddling with it. On the Web, you can alter your product or promotion daily by measuring responses and tweaking as you go. Use this ability to make quick changes that constantly improve your Web site's business "performance."

As you've read, the Microsoft CarPoint Web site supplies information to people in the market for a new car. The site includes a great interactive feature that allows a user to specify the kind of car and options (Nissan Sentra, BMW 318i, air-conditioning, sunroof, etc.), and CarPoint supplies the dealer invoice price. The system is intelligent. For example, if you ask for the "Eddie Bauer" edition of the Ford Explorer and then ask to add leather seats, the service will tell you that leather seats are already included in that package. Users can also trade off options based on how much they cost to put together a car that meets their budget. The resulting price list gives consumers a great bargaining tool to use when they go to a dealer.

CarPoint's designer, Loren Imes, wanted to make this "option swapping" feature easy to use and extremely flexible. For each car, he designed a page that showed basic invoice prices for each model. From there, users could click on a button to get to the interactive feature that allowed them to mix and match options. But because the choice wasn't obvious or prominent, few people realized there was an interactive feature there at all.

Fortunately, as with any Web site, the team could tell this was happening by the number of hits the interactive feature's Web page was getting compared to the number of hits the pages with the basic prices were getting. Of every hundred visitors to the base-price page, only five would go to the interactive pricing engine. Loren knew that consumers wanted to find the price of various options, so he figured that the pricing feature might be too hard to find. A redesign of the page highlighted the customized price list, and the use of that feature skyrocketed. A little observation and redesign made a drastic improvement.

The same scenario presented itself again when the team decided to take their information-only business a step further and help people actually purchase a car. At first they wanted to present this option to consumers subtly. They didn't want to look like ... well ... a pushy car salesman. So on the home page of their Web site, they included the button as a choice among a list of other buttons down the left side of the page. The other buttons offered choices like "car photo gallery" or an article on snow tires. The team was so subtle that the buying option got completely lost in the clutter. Few users used the service to buy a car.

Well, being subtle to avoid looking like a car salesman was one thing, but losing potential business was another. Loren moved the "New Car Buying Source" button to a more prominent spot on the page and made it bigger. He also added the phrase "save money and save time" right under the button. Subtle it was not. He also removed some of the other things on the home page that didn't seem to add much value or weren't very popular. These relatively minor changes focused people on the few things left on the page, especially the car-buying option. The number of consumers who found and used the car-buying service increased substantially.

The following may seem like easy things to do on your Web site, but you would be surprised at how many designers forget these simple rules:

- Choose just a few visual elements or choices for each page. And, don't make graphics so big that the screen takes forever to appear. Users lose patience and go elsewhere.
- Give visual prominence to the things that you want the user to do most or that the user will find most useful or compelling.
- Don't make users wade through a variety of pages to get to important information. The more clicks you require, the higher the likelihood they'll abandon the process.

Three Things I Learned about Hiring People to Work on Your Web Site

CJ Liu Rosenblatt, Business Development Manager,
Interactive Media Division:

1. There's a debate: hire the techie or hire the person coming from the entertainment industry.

   A veteran of the TV, movie, or advertising world may be supercreative, perfect for thinking about the media aspect of the site. But she may not understand the technology. If she doesn't understand what today's tools can do or not do, she won't know what products she can (or can't) create. The techie on the other hand, will know how to build everything, but might lack the training to create a visually compelling user experience. I've found the best team has a mix...mostly techie with a dash of the creatives.

2. You will become what you hire.

   You may be thrilled to hear the latest hiring news that a celebrated mucky-muck or midlevel manager is coming over from a company with a household name. But they can bring a big-company mentality. They've been successful in a world of processes and procedures—that's how they're used to doing things. Web teams need to act quickly without the encumbrances of a heavily linked management chain. These veterans might introduce more analysis and bureaucracy than you can afford in Internet time.

3. Make tough staffing decisions early.

   If you've found you've made a hiring mistake, admit it early and let the person go. They probably aren't any happier about their performance than you are. Don't send them to another group where "their skills might be a better match."

USE YOUR CUSTOMER CONTACTS

In the old days (three years ago), when customers had a product improvement, idea, or complaint, they'd decide to write a letter to the company. But more often than not, the letter would go unwritten. By the time they had typed it up, found the company's address, and labeled the envelope, it hardly seemed worth the effort.

Now we have the Internet. Customers can send E-mail in a flash, capturing their ideas and emotions as they happen. Sending information to a company might only take five minutes. Making your company easy to contact via E-mail can garner great results from surprising customer ideas, to quick notification of problems, to more loyal customers.

The Microsoft Expedia travel service sometimes receives a hundred feature suggestions per day according to Rich Barton, its general manager. One user asked for a way to check to see if an airplane was arriving on time. The team named this feature "Grandma's Flight" for folks who wanted to make sure they got to the airport by the time grandma was getting off the plane. The change was easy to implement, and Expedia met a customer need that they had never thought of. Grandma's Flight, now known as Flight Info, is used thousands of times per day, and is a feature that sets Expedia apart from the other Internet travel agencies.

For Microsoft's Internet magazine, *Slate*, customer contact translates to quick corrections. In a print magazine, a reader may find a mistake, notify the magazine, and see a correction buried somewhere in the next issue. In the meantime, the incorrect data remains out in circulation. With Web-based magazines and other information, the reader sees the error faster, notifies the errant creator, and the mistake can be corrected immediately.

The ease of communication increases the frequency of reader response. Mike Kinsley notes that when he was the editor of

The New Republic magazine, he received thirty reader letters in a busy mail week. As editor of *Slate,* Mike receives fifty per *day* via E-mail (and up to two hundred per day if a controversial topic is covered). The ease of communication also encourages a wider array of contact. The grammar police of the print-magazine world ("Hey, you ended a sentence with a preposition!") have given way to folks who just want to debate a point. Tim Noah wrote a *Slate* article about the Pentagon's naming the latest Iraq bombing Operation Desert Fox: Didn't they know/care that was the nickname of a Nazi general? Within hours he was receiving E-mail from readers contesting his assertion that Rommel was a *Nazi,* rather than a *German,* general.

FREE SAMPLES ON THE WEB

The Web is a great way to offer free samples—from information to services to software products to games. Post the
sample once and let people "take one" for a limited time. Let
them try what you're offering at no risk, then give them an
option to upgrade from the sample to the real thing. Or give
out passwords to allow people to use your whole Web site,
but only for a limited time. Entice them into your product family. Even if your product isn't electronic, the Web gives you
ways to deliver it to customers who are interested.

Microsoft has always been a big believer in free samples. Corporations considering large purchases regularly get thousands
of dollars of free software to try. Trainers and consultants
who support Microsoft products are also often given free
samples of the products to help them keep up on the latest
releases and to encourage them to keep supporting that product line. Microsoft has taken this belief and made it a way of
doing business on the Web. On its Web site (as of this writing), the list of free downloads has ninety-one entries. These
downloads include trial versions, add-on products, and
updates. They range from scaled-down try-before-you-buy
versions of software to monthly movie reviews to kids games
to screen savers to Windows NT technical aids. And that list
doesn't even include the Microsoft Network and its products
and services.

Money Central, the Web site that lets you manage your
portfolio and personal finances, lets users cancel their subscrip-
tion within the first thirty days to avoid ever seeing a bill.
Other products and services take a different twist. The Encarta
encyclopedia posts a free "one-book concise encyclopedia" on
the Web for anyone to use. It lacks many of the features and
the depth of the full-blown product, but it gives users a good

idea of what they'd get in a bigger version. There's also a thirty-day free trial to use the Encarta Deluxe complete version with the opportunity to buy the CD-ROM version or subscribe to the Deluxe on-line version for a year.

A product like Encarta makes its money from the CD-ROM version. Many people, including executives at the company, asked, "Aren't you cannibalizing your own critical CD-ROM sales by offering it on-line?" Vice President Robbie Bach responds, "I'd rather we obsolete ourselves before someone else does. The Internet is the fastest-growing medium. We're just making sure we have a foot in the next generation of products and technology." The same can be said for CD-ROM games that move to the on-line world—especially when the on-line world offers so much more to game players in the form of interaction with a constant stream of new opponents to play against.

You may think your service or product isn't downloadable over the Web, but think again. If you are a banking, consulting, training, or other personal service, you can allow users to post questions to your experts on-line and answer them to demonstrate your knowledge of their situation. You could also point them to appropriate case studies you've written about people with similar issues. If you have a product that can't be delivered over the Web, such as art supplies, or perhaps you own a restaurant or dry cleaner, you can still offer "free samples." When users surf your Web site or strike up an electronic conversation with you, E-mail them a coupon. Think creatively to overcome the electronic barrier. These customers have sought you out and you can communicate personally with them. Do it!

YOUR WEB SITE: SPACE FOR QUIET READING OR PLACE TO GET THINGS DONE?

You've put great data, enticing product information, and terrific sales materials on your Web site. Don't stop there. Let customers take action. For example, consider people who read for pleasure. What would they find more useful—a Web site review of the best-sellers, or that same book review with the opportunity to click a button to buy one of the books? And which would you find more profitable?

The Microsoft CarPoint Web site made this progression from information to selling, little by little. The team always knew it wanted to sell cars over the Internet, but felt that offering information to attract customers was the best way to get established. When it first went on-line, CarPoint displayed data on a variety of cars. It did have some interactive capabilities, but these were limited. For example, users could specify what they were looking for in a car—big load capacity, air bags, room for six, etc.—and get a list of possible matches to their criteria. They could then order a more complete report on any car for six dollars.

The team adopted a concept called "information as retail." A seller usually has to set up an attractive storefront with walls, aisles, and products. On the Web, the CarPoint team felt that offering vital and interesting information was analogous—a cost to set up the business and attract people. Over time, the CarPoint team improved the information and format of the site so customers could do a side-by-side comparison of features, prices, and other data while they were on-line. Customers could really get something done now because they could go to the site and make an informed decision on what car to buy. A plus for the team would be increased traffic at the site, which would in turn attract more advertisers who would pay for space.

The site was improving, but it still only offered information. The next logical step was to include a dealer network so people could buy a car once they finished their research. Customers thought this was great—no hassles and haggles at the dealership. The car sellers were thrilled to reach a whole new audience. CarPoint charged them to be part of the network. Now, CarPoint didn't have to rely on selling ad space on their site and $6 copies of car information pamphlets. They were a partner of a major transaction.

Once the CarPoint team moved from providing information to the more lucrative area of making transactions, they added financing, insurance, and other car-related sales to their site by hooking up with a variety of suppliers and partners. The transition has been a success. In the past three years, the site has grown so it now represents $300 million in car sales—1 percent of all cars sold in the United States.

Unfortunately, redesigning the content of a Web site to work with someone selling something is not a universal panacea. You need to stick with your core competencies and know what your users want. A small Web-based newsmagazine created a feature on travel so they could hook up with the Microsoft Expedia travel-booking service. Perhaps they reasoned that an interesting article on a great travel destination might spark someone's impulse to buy a plane ticket. Or maybe that people in the mood to travel would be likely to search out this section and then buy a plane ticket. The magazine would be paid a few dollars for each referral of a customer who bought a plane ticket on Expedia. Sadly, their editorial effort netted less than one thousand dollars per month from Expedia, which was probably less than they paid writers to create the travel articles in the first place. The readers of the magazine were looking for breaking news, not travel-destination descriptions. The pair-up didn't fly.

Three Lessons I've Learned about Doing Business on the Web

Rogers Weed, Director of Marketing,
Windows CE

1. **Lots of people think, "The Web changes everything." It does change a lot, but the basics of good business still apply.**
   A compelling product, excellent customer service, and a reliable distribution system are as critical as ever.
2. **There is no "field of dreams."**
   Just because you build it doesn't mean they'll come. You still need to generate awareness using PR, advertising, and promotions.
3. **Don't overtinker your Web site.**
   It's great to be able to change this and that to make your Web site more exciting or more useful. Just don't get so wrapped up in those details that you miss thinking about your overall strategy.

BUILDING YOUR COMMUNITY

Want to exchange serious thoughts on your favorite *Star Trek* episode or the latest naturopathic treatments? Where else could you find twenty people to play some obscure medieval game with you at 4:35 A.M.? There's always someone on the Internet ready to chat, play, or exchange information. The Web is a unique combination of software and socializing. If you enhance that feeling of being part of a community, you can build loyalty to your site and your products. As Pierre Omidyar, billionaire founder of Ebay, the on-line auction service, told the *New York Times,* "I thought people would simply use the service to buy and sell things, but what they really enjoyed was meeting other people."

The Microsoft Gaming Zone is a Web site where people come to play games against other people, and each of the games is a separate "product" designed by Microsoft or another company. But Microsoft saw the Gaming Zone itself as a product and assigned a whole staff of designers to the Web site.

While some of the designers work on the games, another group works solely on creating an atmosphere, information, and events that will engage users. If users enjoy themselves, they stay longer, return more often, and bring their friends. This design team is a bit like the *Love Boat*'s cruise director, Julie McCoy. They make sure that people have the opportunity to meet and have fun together.

To meet this goal, the team added some special touches to the site. For example, when players finish a game, they can publicly post their score. This has created a whole series of challenges and ongoing rivalries as gamers try to top each other. Next are "tournaments" that invite people to show up at a certain time to compete at a specified game. Sometimes the Microsoft Zone Team takes on any challengers or sets up a public match with writers from a gaming magazine. Users can log on to "watch" the match and cheer for their team. The designers also created "dossiers" or different personalities people can assume when they enter the site. Offered multiple personas, gamers can play in whatever mood they find themselves. Competitions, spectator events, and the ability to chat with other players have made the site a hit.

Other products take different approaches to creating a community, depending on the personalities and needs of their customers. *Slate* magazine, which covers current events and political news, hosts on-line forums that only subscribers can attend. The subscribers figure they are better informed than the average Joe, so they like their talks to be restricted, creating more of a clublike atmosphere.

One of the ways the Windows team created a community was by letting users post technical dilemmas to other users. It's a great way for customers to quickly get answers to problems that other folks have faced. The Windows group has also found that some of their customers like to hang out on-line and become known as the "guy who solves all the technical problems." People often get as much out of giving information or help as they do by receiving it.

Encarta helps kids K–12 find more Web sites and sources of information for their school projects and papers from a professional researcher. The site also lets kids meet pen pals and "stay safe on-line." These extra services, tangentially related to the encyclopedia itself, make kids happy and their parents more comfortable with the site.

Examining the likes and needs of your on-line community will start you on the road to providing them an informative and convivial place to go on the Web. As you do this, don't forget your potential customers—the community you hope to attract in the future. Do they like to exchange information, compete, or just find a shoulder to cry on? Look at ways to design your site to let these things happen.

THERE IS NO MANUFACTURING...
OR IS THERE?

Companies get excited about providing information over the Web, thinking, "There's no manufacturing!" Magazines can post articles in cyberspace instead of printing them on paper. Hotels can take reservations and don't have to print or send a brochure. Users can just go up to the Web and download information. It's free to them and free to the company providing it. No manufacturing, right? Not quite.

"You can't sell anything if the store isn't open," says Rich Barton, general manager of the Expedia travel-planning Web site at Microsoft. "On the Web, manufacturing equates to the critical assurance that your Web site is up and running." Does your technology ensure that you are open seven days a week, twenty-four hours a day? Will you be alerted if something breaks down? Do you have the capacity to deliver your information as the number of users on the Internet grows?

When the technical aspects are nailed down, move to the practical. How are people going to use your site? Do you have all the appropriate information available? Or are you going to lead people halfway to a sale via the Net and then make them call you anyway because you lack a key data point such as volume pricing or the nearest dealership? What controls are in place to make sure you are alerted if the site experiences a snafu?

Barton has set up the equivalent of factory managers for his Web site. He has a director of operations whose sole responsibility is the health of the engine and the technology that supports the Expedia site. Rich also keeps tabs on the site with a simple transaction counter.

As Expedia sells airline tickets, he receives a message via his PC. For every hundred tickets sold, the message prompts the

PC to make the sound of a bell ringing (like the opening of the stock market). For every thousand tickets sold, he hears applause coming from his PC *and* he receives a page on the pager he always wears (okay, he is a little obsessive.) But perhaps more useful, he has a screen that shows how many tickets have been sold for that day (by the minute) and how many were sold yesterday, as well as the week-to-date and the prior week's sales. He can also slice and dice the data, check on current promotions, and perform a variety of other calculations. By monitoring this, Rich and his team can see if the numbers are slowing down. If they do, that's a signal something may be wrong on the site.

ADVERTISING: NO TIME TO BE CUTE

The Web offers up a great advertising opportunity. Moving pictures and words make the ads more dynamic than those static ones that sit lamely on a printed page. And, Web ads are much cheaper than their counterparts on TV. But people's attention span may even be shorter—if that is possible—on the Web. Most of the time, the page they're clicking on is just part of the path to get to their destination. If your message isn't tight, short, and compelling, they're likely to click away to the next place on the Web before you even get a chance to show it all.

The Expedia travel service learned this lesson the hard way. They had a clever ad with a powerful message. It went something like this:

Want to buy a ticket to Minneapolis?
Nonstop?
With a window seat?
And a kosher meal?
That's all?
(Visually shows how the product works.)
Microsoft Expedia, with flight wizard
Plan Travel
Book Travel
Go Travel
Click Here

Each sentence appeared after the previous one disappeared, building excitement as the ad revealed the great offer. The problem was, customers never made it to the last step. They had no time to sit through the slow-moving ad and just blew past it on their way to something else. Shortening and tightening the same idea to just:

Plan Travel
Book Travel
Go Travel
Click Here

yielded a snappier ad that pulled people into the site.

Microsoft's Link Exchange gives a better example of getting the message across quickly. Link Exchange is a service on the Web that allows sites to swap links with other sites. For example, a car maker and an insurance company might trade links. Each would advertise on the other's Web property, and each would allow customers to bounce between them. Link Exchange's ad simply said, "Want people to see your Web site? Click here to find out how." The only visual was the logo. The message was snappy, self-explanatory, and targeted the right audience.

In a related note, a cute stunt or word used just to attract people, without a targeted message, will likely be a waste of your time and money. Some Web site owners try to entice customers to their site with spicy little ads that say "free sex" or something else that's either provocative or funny. But once customers click to the site, they realize that the offer or the joke or whatever it was that grabbed them has nothing to do with the actual site. They quickly leave. Web site owners think, "Oh, I've attracted lots of people to the site. See how many clicked on my ad to find me on the Web?" But more often then not, they've wasted their advertising dollars because they've targeted the wrong group entirely.

The Internet and people's PCs are still so slow that people are eager to move on as soon as they have the option. They're also probably on the Web for a specific purpose such as finding information or buying a gift. Creating a concise ad that truly targets potential customers will yield the greatest number of appropriate users visiting you on the Web.

COMMUNICATING WITH NETIQUETTE

Doing business on the Web means E-mail and lots of it. Customers, coworkers, press people, hired agencies, are all more likely to pick up a keyboard than a phone to contact you. "Let your fingers do the walking" has a new meaning now.

E-mail can be a strange way of communicating. You can have a conversation with someone, one sentence at a time, over the course of a week. You can vent your frustrations without looking the person in the eye or hearing his or her reaction. You can send an incredibly romantic thought... to the wrong person.

Use these eight quick E-mail guidelines to stay out of trouble and get the most out of your outbox.

KEEP YOUR OUTGOING E-MAILS
TO ONE SCREENFUL

Short E-mail is good E-mail. Many folks on the receiving end will open an E-mail message, start to scan, and if it goes on past one screen, will close it up to read when they have more time. "When they have more time" may be at the dawn of the next ice age. The same goes for "attachments"—documents, spreadsheets, and presentations embedded in or attached to the mail. Opening up an E-mail and getting assaulted with a string of attachments to access, read, or print is too daunting for most people to embark on at first sight. These messages are closed quickly, almost fearfully, and may never get reopened.

You *can* use the long E-mail chock-full of embedded documents to your advantage. Bury a funding proposal in the appendix of an attachment in the middle of a ten-screen E-mail. On page 10 type, "If I do not hear from you in one week, I will consider this approved." Of course, you should plan to use this strategy only once.

USE YOUR SUBJECT LINE

Make your subject line or header a brief, clear description of the contents of the message. Due dates and "action required" are good attention-getters. They also can dramatically reduce the instances of "Oh, I didn't notice you wanted a response." "PR action items" and "2/18 meeting notes" are good examples of descriptive, concise subject lines. "Why?" "Thanks," and "Information Requested" are not.

Sometimes you can use your subject line in a sneaky way to get someone's attention. I titled one message "Bruce Springsteen Tickets" to a coworker who hadn't responded to my last three E-mails requesting sales data. She opened it right away and was probably surprised to see the sales information request again, but this time she responded. Probably out of guilt. Other subject lines sure to get your message opened quickly are "Your Raise," "Cute New Guy/Gal," and "Layoff Rumors."

BREAK YOUR ADDICTION TO
THE REPLY-ALL BUTTON

E-mail can be a terrific forum for discussions and decisions that replace meetings. Someone will float a proposal, maybe an idea for a new marketing campaign in response to news of a competitor. Or maybe the findings and analysis of the latest research will be sent around. Seeing these messages, you want to pipe in with your two cents. You want to be seen as a participant, a problem solver, a team player!

But save only your top thoughts for the reply-all button. Don't feel that you have to respond to prove you read the mail. Also, sending the words "I agree" to fifty recipients is not a good way to make friends.

And look *really* closely at who is on the reply-all list. At Microsoft, influential industry-magazine editors have been copied by mistake on confidential corporate decisions because, way back on the E-mail thread, their opinion was solicited. Once, during a shifting around of projects and responsibilities, the message "There's no one worth hiring in that group" went to "that group." A major morale slump and fear for the personal safety of the sender resulted.

IT MAY FEEL GOOD TO "FLAME" BUT...

Someone has just sent you a *stupid* E-mail with *incorrect* results from an *idiotic* test that anyone with *half a brain* could have predicted. You'd like to yell at the sender through your keyboard using ALL CAPS and lots of those symbols: @$#^@%$. Wait. Take a breath. Take another. Don't send that flame mail! Breathe. Read the message again. Sometimes you've misunderstood something in your reading haste. If you flame *and* you're wrong, you will not only look like a reactionary, but a stupid reactionary for not even understanding the E-mail.

Okay, you've read it again and it truly makes you furious for good reason. Reply calmly. Try "Are you sure that data is correct?" or "I believe you may have meant..." The sender may actually have a good explanation. Or they may have made a mistake in the mail. Or, they may truly be stupid, an HR hiring mistake, but what good will it do to make them feel bad about that? You may even need a favor from them one day. So don't go medieval on them unless it's really, truly necessary.

If you disregard the above and decide to flame anyway, please don't copy tons of people on the mail. Not only will the flamed one think you are a jerk for doing the equivalent of yelling at him or her electronically, with many virtual witnesses to the drubbing, but the other recipients will likely think, "Well, yeah, that was a stupid E-mail...but what a mean response!" These virtual witnesses will not be on your side—they will be imagining getting roasted one day themselves! They may actually be physically cringing as they read.

DON'T CLOG THE SYSTEM WITH
HUGE ATTACHMENTS

Sure you're proud of the presentation you just gave—it's got pictures, sound clips, colors flying across the screen. But your megabyte monster can slow the network to a crawl as you send it to more and more people. And when it leaves the corporation for the real world (a vendor or partner), you can bring their system to its knees. I have personally taken down Microsoft's entire PR firm with a document boasting *every* new Word for Windows software feature, accompanied by a picture.

Stay short and sweet. Extract the real meat from your attachment and put it into your E-mail text. You'll save the recipient's time, the network's resources, and have a better chance of getting the material read. If they really need to see the whole document, you may want to copy it onto a corporate network location and tell them in the mail where they can find it.

DON'T SEND CHAIN LETTERS

You may be threatened with intergalactic invasion if you don't pass the chain E-mail message on to six coworkers. Or be promised a trip to Disneyland from Bill Gates if you do. Don't give in! You've never done it with a paper chain-mail letter, why start now?

Yeah, it's so much easier to forward on to six other E-mail names, rather than the old way of making copies, addressing and licking envelopes. But the math on this puppy can quickly escalate to millions of messages. Millions of messages may require your computer-help desk team or MIS folks to spend their time deleting all the chain mail that is now gunking up the system. Wouldn't you rather have them using their time to solve your real software problems?

Next time this comes around—"Send this to 5 people or your heart will be broken in the next 24 hours. This E-mail has

traveled around the world 50 times in the past 2 weeks, and over 300 couples have broken up. So, if you have ever wanted to fall in love, or if you want to keep whatever you have now..."
—take the risk.

DON'T THINK YOUR CORPORATE E-MAIL IS PRIVATE

E-mail and its contents, as well as any other data stored on or transmitted by company-owned equipment, are usually considered the property of the company. The company may access this data if needed; so the privacy of E-mail and such other data cannot be guaranteed. So don't say or do anything over E-mail that you wouldn't want your boss or mother to see. E-mail has been used in reasons for firing and was of course subpoenaed by the Justice Department in Microsoft's case. If you don't want some government or corporate auditor knowing you're having an affair with your boss's boss, keep it off E-mail!

KEEPING UP WITH LARGE VOLUMES OF E-MAIL (50+/DAY)

Microsofties are inundated with a constant stream of incoming mail. And they have different ways of integrating this ongoing deluge into their workday. Some people read new mail once in the morning and once before they go home. Others read it between each meeting to see if anything urgent has come up in the last hour. Some use it to break up their work—looking at the in-box whenever they need a little change of pace. After all, there may be a joke in there a friend sent over the Internet! But no matter your style, the key to surviving those hundred-plus message days is to stay off any aliases you don't absolutely need to be on, and to deal with each piece of mail the first time you read it.

There are all sorts of aliases: social aliases such as the softball team, interest aliases such as beagle owners, work group aliases such as your team or division alias, news aliases that deliver headlines, competitor or other market information, etc. Join as many as you want at first. Then as your E-mail volume starts to rise, see which have the really valuable information and which you can do without. Cut back as you need.

When you sit down to read your E-mail, do something with each piece. After you read a message, delete it, file it, forward it, or do the action required by the mail, such as reply to it. Don't let it pile up! Messages will get buried and balls dropped. At Microsoft, the most efficient E-mailers keep ten messages in their in-box at a time, to remind them of ten things they still need to do or read. Other folks have five hundred messages. These are usually the people who you need to call on the phone for any response, although they will scan for friends' or executives' names in the headers of new incoming mail and open those.

A stuffed in-box is like a time bomb. Something in there is going to go off and you may be the collateral damage. Before I reformed my E-mailing ways, my boss once asked me, "Where's that data I asked for last week? I need to review it and send it on to the VP." I rifled through my in-box (electronically speaking), and message 287 of the 443 I had did indeed request such data. I spent until 3 A.M. that night scrambling to pull it together, blew off a dinner date, and didn't even do a great job on the report! The next few days saw a major purge session between me and my PC.

CHAPTER 3

New Products

Microsoft managers have launched hundreds of products ranging in sales from the boutique Frank Lloyd Wright CD-ROM to the globally ubiquitous Windows operating system. The straightforward product launch is just about down to a science at Microsoft, sometimes too much so, with schedules, plans, test products, and marketing materials mapped all the way out to eight months before the product gets to stores. The process can be quite daunting.

Despite the structure, managers can sometimes improvise. If the market for their product doesn't seem quite right, they rethink what they're offering or team up with another company to deliver something more compelling. If their promotion flops, they try to figure out why and find another route. Whether they're charting new territory or following in someone else's footsteps, the best leaders listen to new ideas, no matter how odd. And when there are hard choices to make, they get their whole team involved.

WHAT A DUMB IDEA? YOU MIGHT NOT BE THE RIGHT PERSON TO MAKE THAT STATEMENT

"I'm the manager, so if I don't like an idea from my team, it shouldn't get done."

Before you start shooting down ideas that you think won't work, ask yourself a critical question. Are you supposed to like the idea? Are you the target audience? If you are a thirty-year-old woman, you probably won't like the video game designed for a teenage boy. If you feel that public television is the only valuable programming on TV, you may not be the best person to evaluate a network's latest sitcom. Evaluate the idea based on what you know about its intended audience, not on your personal biases.

At a product review for Microsoft's word-processing software, Word, a designer excitedly presented a radical change in the way files were stored and opened. He explained to those present, including the division vice president, that the group had run extensive tests and surveys. They found that millions of people used the part of the product they intended to change, and improving the features would be a big win. The improvements would make the computer work more like a human, rather than force the human to think like the computer.

The VP looked at the product team and the product designer and dismissed the idea by snapping, "Well...I don't use it."

The room was silent. The product designer was put in the unenviable position of having to challenge his boss's boss's boss. Knowing that the idea was valid, he pursued it, saying, "Yes, but you are one person."

"Yes, but I still don't use it," the VP said to the silent and visibly uncomfortable group.

The product designer persevered: "This improvement saves customers a few seconds every time they use the product. With ninety percent market share, and ninety-five percent of those people using this feature, if we improve it ten percent we could practically raise the GNP of America." That was enough to make the obstinate VP laugh, breaking the tension, so the product designer forged ahead, presenting the research more seriously.

The VP finally got the point and agreed to the changes. (You may ask how he got to be a VP. That's a different lesson.) The changes in the product were a success with customers. In fact, other teams at Microsoft, such as the Windows NT team, incorporated the same technology in *their* products.

So, before you blurt out, "That's the dumbest idea I've ever heard," stop and remember who is likely to purchase the product or service. Don't be afraid to go with an idea you don't like personally as long as it meets your customers' needs. As long as you have researched the real target audience, you shouldn't be too far off the mark.

Lessons I've Learned about Presenting a New Idea

Michael Hebert, former director of Microsoft Office:

1. **Most people think they're prepared if they have the data supporting every statement they make.**

   If you really want to be thorough, know the methodology used to get that data too! When you know how the study was done (focus groups of new customers, in-store interviews of people who bought competitive products, random digit dialing, etc.) and you really believe in it, you can field almost any question regarding its results.

2. **Simplify your whole approach to center on the top two or three questions you really need to answer. Ignore the dogs and ponies.**

   You may know all details of the situation, but not everyone in the room needs to learn them too. Think about the time-crunched managers whose approval you need. Concise and compelling leaves a stronger impression than exhaustively thorough. Focus on what will have the most impact.

CHANGE THE CENTER OF GRAVITY

You may think of your product as an ingredient, add-on, or accessory to another product. For example, baking soda is generally used as an ingredient for cookies, pies, and cakes. To sell well, baking soda had to be formulated to perform that function successfully. Using a planet-sun analogy, the baking soda is like a planet in the universe where baked goods are like the sun. This all sounds a little woo-woo, but bear with me for a second. An attitude stems from this supposed relationship that if baked goods went out of fashion or recipes ceased calling for baking soda, the demand for it would disappear.

This is a valid point of view but one that holds the "planet" product hostage and subject to the fortunes of its sun. Why shouldn't the planet also view itself as having its own center of gravity? Can't it be used on its own, sold for a different purpose, or combined with something else? When Arm & Hammer baking soda went from a cake ingredient to a fridge freshener, and to a toothpaste ingredient, it changed its center of gravity. All this half-baked analogy is to say, don't take for granted the set of circumstances you are given.

When Jon Roberts became a general manager of Windows CE, he saw the area as an offshoot to Microsoft's main Windows franchise. Windows CE is a smaller, simpler version of the company's flagship operating system. It is designed for portable devices such as phones, radios, and handheld electronic organizers. Since Jon had come from the main Windows group, he saw CE from that group's perspective. This "little" product was just an extension to Windows—a way to connect PCs running the "real" windows to smaller devices. With this connection for example, a PC could download a schedule to an electronic personal organizer or a phone could transmit data to a PC.

As Jon analyzed his business, he asked a litany of questions:

- Who is going to use this technology and when will these products be ready to sell?
- What is the business model? Who are the competitors?
- What are our competitive advantages?
- Who is going to distribute our products?
- What is the vision five years out into the future?

At the back of his mind, Jon knew something wasn't quite right. He kept thinking of customer scenarios that didn't quite fit the model of "Windows CE is an extension to the PC." If someone was driving a car, getting directions to a destination via a global positioning system, no PC would be involved. If a person wanted his or her cell phone to dial itself using the address book from his or her electronic organizer, no PC would be involved. So then Jon asked a different question: "Are we even focused on the right problem?"

Jon realized that Windows CE could be the center of its own universe. It was more than simply an offshoot of Windows. Changing this mind-set changed the "center of gravity," i.e., things could revolve around CE. CE wasn't just tied to its big brother, Windows. Technologies, devices, partnerships, could all be done independently of Windows. Changing the center of gravity gave the team the freedom to expand CE into new devices and customer scenarios, such as smart cards (like corporate security cards) and "universal plug and play," which is a technology effort to connect all kinds of devices, not necessarily just those running Windows.

Changing the center of gravity can also be manifested in the way you do business. In the mid-nineties, customers wanted to link together computers that were using Windows NT to achieve "back-end server synchronization." It doesn't really matter what that is; what does matter is that a small, relatively unknown company offered a product to do it. Although the product worked well, large corporate customers didn't want to trust the health of their vital PC networks to a small company that might be out of business in a year or two. For its part, Microsoft wanted this product to be available because it helped the sales of the Windows NT product.

A buyout of the small company would have appeased corporate customers because Microsoft would then own and continue to support the product. However, the cost of buying the company and integrating it into Microsoft was greater than Microsoft wanted to pay to shore up a small niche market.

Rather than be bound to the usual "make vs. buy" decision, Microsoft and the other company changed the center of gravity. They simply made a deal where Microsoft would answer the service calls for the small company. Microsoft benefited because a great product was available at a manageable cost to work with its Windows NT software. The small company saw its sales jump because it was associated with Microsoft, but it still kept its independence. And customers were happy that they now had one phone number that put them in touch with technical support for any network-related problems. They had the technology from the small company *and* the support and long-term backing of Microsoft.

RIGHT TARGET AND THE RIGHT TIME

You may spend lots of time and money to determine your target audience. Who will buy your product? What benefits are going to appeal to them? What is their age, gender, and psychographic situation? After lots of researching and thinking, you'll usually find your group and decide the message you want to convey to them vis-à-vis your product or service. But remember to choose the time of that delivery carefully. Make sure people are in the right place, the right time, and the right mind-set to hear what you have to say.

In January of 1996, Microsoft Internet Explorer (IE) had a two percent share of the Internet browser market. An Internet browser is a piece of software that allows customers to get on the Web and "surf" (or browse, hence the name, browser) the Web. The IE marketing team wanted to make a big splash with a new upgrade of the product. They reasoned that the market was so small, and Microsoft's part in it so minuscule, that even a small boost among influential users would be a good thing.

Microsoft is not known for doing things in a subtle way, and the IE group was no exception. After discussion of possible high-profile places to find customers, the team decided to put a CD-ROM of Internet Explorer on every seat...of the Super Bowl. It's the right target, they reasoned. The fans in those seats would be more likely to be upper income, well educated, and male. These fans epitomized the 1996 demographic profile of an Internet user.

The team also envisioned rubbing elbows with CEOs and TV stars, and striking up a conversation about Internet Explorer. Indeed, a couple of the marketers got tickets on the fifty-yard line with the mucky-mucks. One of them, Yusuf Mehdi, at the time a junior product manager, even sat next to Anthony

Edwards, Dr. Greene on the hit TV show *ER*. Heady stuff for someone still in his twenties. But one thing the team forgot to consider was that no one at the Super Bowl was interested in talking about computers. "They basically wanted to drink beer and watch the game," Yusuf said, "as you might imagine."

In addition to the CD-ROM, the marketing team targeted the pregame VIP area for scintillating conversations about IE. There, they set up PCs connected to the Internet so the VIPs could check out pregame statistics and player chats, as well as the first-ever NFL on-line "webcast," which ran during the actual game.

Sadly for the Microsoft zealots, the participants didn't want to bother with these crazy computer folks when they had the chance to time their speed on the forty-yard dash. Almost no one went home and tried out their free Internet Explorer CD-ROM. The promotion was a complete flop (except for the team members who got the great seats to the Super Bowl) and extremely expensive.

When you're targeting your audience of potential buyers, make sure they are in the frame of mind to receive your message. A dog-food demonstration will probably go over better at a dog show than among a dog-breeder group having their quarterly lunch together. Free samples of your chocolate may be a great idea, but don't set up your stand next to the health food store. The where, when, and how of the message delivery is just as critical as the who.

INTEGRATION DAY

Sometimes there's no substitute for propinquity. No matter how clear you make your plan, the implementations of your ideas and instructions won't be coordinated unless, well, you coordinate them. No one likes meeting just for meeting's sake, but getting everyone in the same room has its benefits. This is especially true for groups who won't share daily contact as their project progresses. Invest the time and money early to develop a shared foundation so the parts of your promotion, product, or plan are working in synchronicity.

Jharna Jain's first assignment as a marketer (she had switched from the technical side of the company) was to plan the launch of Microsoft's new software that would help people prepare and file their taxes. In her new job, she diligently did her research to establish the appropriate target market and to develop a compelling consumer promise. She mapped out the messages she wanted to relay to customers and divvied out her marketing budget in a preliminary marketing plan.

Jharna handed out this introductory marketing plan with its budgets, targets, and messages to the leaders of her specialty teams, including public relations, advertising, and distribution. She wanted them to organize more detailed marketing activities in their specific areas of expertise based on the plan. Jharna reasoned that if they each had the same goals, customer, and competitive information, their individual strategies would all make sense and work together.

Jharna was surprised when she received the reports back from her PR, advertising, and distribution teams. Even though they were all working off the same information, which she felt detailed who the customer was and what Microsoft wanted to say, each of the areas was taking a different approach to the marketing. One team organized a national campaign while another chose a regional approach. Another veered slightly off the prioritization of the messages to make their campaign more creative. Each team had done their best, but that best effort was being done in a vacuum. They didn't know what the other teams were thinking.

To get the teams going in the right direction, Jharna held an "integration day." She brought the groups together to discuss ideas and to make sure they agreed on the basics: target market, message priorities, and budget weighting.

As each team presented their plan, the other teams readjusted their thinking to create synergies rather than each doing their own thing. The distribution folks talked about concentrating on certain regional stores and partnering with them to create a big product splash. The budget wasn't big, so the distribution team argued for getting strong partners and covering "a few cities well" rather than a widespread and thinly covered national rollout.

"I agree with the distribution team's approach, trying to concentrate on a few cities rather than go national," Jem from the advertising team commented. The distribution team nodded. "I guess we should do regional ads in those newspapers rather than pay for a national ad that won't be backed up by any other elements of the marketing mix," he continued. Everyone in the room started nodding, and Jharna felt a huge wave of relief as she saw the team start to bounce ideas off each other. The advertising team would say, "If you send out direct mail, we can coordinate radio ads the same week." Or distribution would suggest, "Get those local ads to say, 'Buy it at the CompUSA store,' and I'll ask CompUSA to pay for half the ads."

The expert groups discussed the messages and priorities together so their coordinated ads and PR would carry the same slogans. They saw how they could each play off the other to get more impact from their own piece of the work. After a few hours of brainstorming they actually wanted to do things similarly, rather than each concentrating on their own unique implementation of the ideas. They slowly morphed into a team focused on the same goals.

A CORE BUSINESS WILL BE
JEALOUSLY GUARDED

Don't just examine the size, strength, or number of your potential competitors. Before you enter a new market, determine
the importance of success to your business rivals. Is this a side
business for them with little effect on their company's income?
Or is it the strategic key to their existence? Companies will
fight hard to protect key assets, key revenue streams, key
relationships. If a competitor can't afford to lose, know you're
going to have to work a lot harder to win.

In 1995, Microsoft's hardware division found the market ripe
for an interactive toy (i.e., a toy with a computer chip that
could respond to a child, videotape, and computer software).
More families were purchasing PCs. Kids were comfortable
using computers for games and homework. Toys were becoming more sophisticated. The hardware division at that time
made mice, keyboards, joysticks, and a kid's "pointing device"
(basically a big trackball version of a mouse). They had expertise in hardware/software interaction and knew how to test
products and software with kids to ensure the products were
usable. Talented mechanical and electrical engineers staffed the
invention team. Microsoft purchased a small (five-person) company, Dare to Dream, with a great idea. The market was ready,
and now, so was Microsoft.

What the hardware division lacked was any knowledge or
experience in the toy business. They knew Christmas was the
main selling season. They knew some complicated buying/rec-
ommending patterns existed between kids, peers, parents, and
teachers. But they didn't really have good contacts for distributing, merchandising, or promoting a toy.

Recognizing this, Microsoft went to Hasbro and Mattel to
form partnerships. Those companies, however, eschewed any

type of alliance. They decided they could make their own interactive toy if they wanted to and didn't need Microsoft software engineers telling them how to do it.

Without a toy company to partner with, Microsoft went off on its own. The team created an interactive plush doll of Barney the purple dinosaur, heartthrob of the two-year-old crowd. It played peekaboo when you covered its eyes, sang songs when you squeezed its hands, and played games when you squeezed its feet.

Microsoft's Barney responded and communicated with computer software and videos. It also interacted with live broadcasts of the Barney TV show—another first. It became one of the best-selling toys of the 1997 Christmas selling season (no. 4 among all plush toys and no. 23 of all traditional toys), taking the major toy companies by surprise.

The next year, Microsoft used the same concept and technology to create interactive dolls of the popular animated kids characters Arthur and D.W. That Christmas, interactive dolls flooded the market from a variety of companies. Most were hard for kids to figure out or had a fairly uninteresting feature set. They didn't have some of the thoughtful touches Microsoft's had. For instance, when a child played with the Microsoft Arthur software, without the doll, the Arthur character would show up on the screen to give instructions. When the doll was being used with the software, the character didn't appear on the screen because it was sitting with the child and talking. Still, the Microsoft toys sold much more poorly than the year before.

Why? During that Christmas selling season, the toy companies brought so many resources to bear on the market that Arthur and D.W. got lost in the sea of interactives—Winnie the Pooh, Furby, and a relaunched Teddy Ruxpin. Mattel and Hasbro were battling back, refusing to let Microsoft get a foothold in their business.

Christmas and the retail toy channel can make or break the profitability of a toy company. Those companies use enormous marketing budgets to try to start a buzz and make a toy hot. The companies even hire "fluffers," people who go into retail stores to check on stocking levels and tidy up displays of their products. Christmas retail is the core, the heart and soul of a toy company—this is where they make every effort to win. They wouldn't be caught short again this year by interloper Microsoft in the new interactive toy category.

Other factors made the companies even tougher to compete with. Toy companies often buy a license to a character like Winnie the Pooh and spread that licensing cost across a number of products including plush toys, action figures, backpacks, and lunch boxes. If one item flops, the others can absorb costs or make up the revenue shortfall. Also, lines of products can afford pricing strategies. For example, Nintendo can discount one cartridge in a series and take a loss, to get kids hooked on the series as a whole. Microsoft only had three toys, so there wasn't much room to spread risk or cost.

Toy companies can't afford to lose to competitors in their core business, so they assemble all their energy to succeed there. In contrast, the two hundred employees of the Microsoft hardware division focus on PC peripherals and business customers to provide their main source of income. Hardware makers and software stores are important to them, not toy stores. Barney and his interactive cohorts were a tiny part of the division's profits. If there were extra resources or dollars available to the division as a whole, there'd probably be a more effective place for them than to fight toy-market leader Mattel at Toys " Я " Us.

Microsoft had the technology to create a good toy but didn't have the ability or desire to focus enough resources on its success. To win in the toy business, a company has to fund a high-dollar marketing campaign every year to make the toy noticed during the key selling season. Microsoft wasn't able to support this. Because there was less at stake for Microsoft, Microsoft was also less committed. Because toys aren't their core business, the management didn't want to divert more horsepower to attempt success in the toy channel.

An interesting end note here. Before the 1998 Christmas season was over, the toy companies realized they did indeed need software expertise to create high-quality interactive products. The ones they had created, for the most part, received poor reviews. Mattel purchased the Learning Company (a software company) to bring some expertise in-house. There's talk of a possible alliance forming between another toy company and Microsoft to possibly license the Barney, Arthur, and D.W. interactive dolls. It looks like the software experts and toy-marketing machine may be joining forces after all. In the meantime, though, Microsoft is still trying to succeed in the toy market with a new entry—interactive Teletubbie dolls. I've seen kids arguing over who gets to play with an early test version of the doll, and another who has adopted the doll as a family member, so I bet they'll do just fine.

TEAMING UP WITH A COMPETITOR
TO ENTER A NEW MARKET

You're about to enter a market segment with a new item or service, or maybe to sell an older product to a new audience. Check out the lay of the land to determine your competitors' strengths and weaknesses. Can you at least match them? Can you do better in a key area?

If they're entrenched, it may not be possible to beat them. If you can't "beat 'em," well, it may actually make sense to "join 'em."

Four years ago, twenty-six-year-old Rich Barton told his bosses that their idea of making travel-guide CD-ROMs was misguided. Rather than selling travel books, he argued that the real money was on the Internet in the form of booking people's travel. His bosses agreed and eventually let him head up the Microsoft venture Expedia, which has become one of the biggest travel agents on the web.* Consumers loved how easy it was to compare hotel prices and airfares, as well as book travel arrangements. Leaping in just four years from a junior marketer to the manager of sixty people and the head of a small enterprise, Rich found it a challenge just to keep up with his growing responsibilities. But he always kept looking for bigger and better growth opportunities for Expedia. The consumer travel sector, which Expedia served, represented billions in yearly sales; however, those sales were made one person and one trip at a time. Another multibillion-dollar segment of the travel-booking industry lay virtually untouched by the Internet—corporate travel.

Many corporations have an official travel agency that obtains group rates for airfares and hotels, books trade-show travel, and arranges for special corporate discounts. When

---

*To find more on this story, check out my first book, *All I Really Need to Know in Business I Learned at Microsoft*.

businesspeople want to book a business trip, they contact their corporate travel agent or perhaps send an E-mail with the dates and destination. The agent checks out their hotel/airline preferences and the latest corporate discounts.

Rich and the Expedia team wanted to sell their service to these corporations, making travel planning possible via computer rather than via travel agent. But breaking into the corporate market would be tough. Big players including American Express, Carlson Wagonlit, Rosenbluth, and Worldwide Travel Partners dominated it, and they would fight hard to keep it.

Rich imagined walking into General Electric, Ford, or other Fortune 500 companies trying to sell them on a travel service from a software company with almost no travel credentials. He figured his prospects were grim. He believed Microsoft did offer superior technology and could improve the travel-booking process, but lacked the credibility to get in the door. So instead of competing directly with his competitors, he decided to team up with one of them.

American Express Travel Services, the biggest player in that market segment, was looking for a way to keep its edge over the competition. By teaming up with Microsoft's Expedia, Amex could adopt the latest technology and gain an important competitive advantage. Other players had implemented a variety of on-line reservation systems, but since technology wasn't their core competency, they had met with mixed to mediocre results. A technology gap waited to be filled.

Expedia and American Express worked together to create a special version of the computerized booking system, and Amex rolled it out to its corporate customers. Instead of calling an agent, a businessperson could now easily log on to a computer and make his or her own reservations. The corporation could set parameters in the system to help keep its employees within a budget. For example, hotel choices could be restricted to a certain price range, and the system could suggest airlines that gave the company the best rates. Rooms could be held for a

trade show and canceled if not booked. Amex gained a technological advantage over the competition, and the Expedia team
used American Express's credentials and existing relationships
(aka distribution) to get their travel technology into businesses
worldwide.

Expedia made a two-year exclusive deal with Amex to use
the electronic booking tool. When that time is up, Microsoft
can sell the reservation system to other big players such as Carlson Wagonlit, Rosenbluth, and Worldwide Travel Partners.
Expedia used its core competency—its technology—to partner
with an established presence to enter the market. Rich and his
team realized they'd make more money by selling their technology to the competitors than by competing alone. In fact, they
didn't really end up competing at all. They can sell the technology to everyone! For its part, Amex gets a two-year technology
jump on the competition, which helps them grow their business.

In another example of teaming with a potential competitor, Microsoft created a remote control to combine all the
other stereo and TV remotes sitting around someone's house.
To sell it, Microsoft would have to branch into electronics
stores and learn about a whole new channel. Instead,
Microsoft partnered with the well-established electronics
company Harmon-Kardon. Harmon-Kardon had the knowledge, the contacts, and the experience in that channel. Their
sales force carried the product into their existing outlets. Harmon-Kardon also guaranteed Microsoft that it would buy a
certain number of units to defray development costs. Again,
Microsoft didn't have to compete with every market leader
for shelf space and didn't have to learn about a whole new
distribution system. Microsoft lowered its risk by teaming up
with an expert in the field.

Please make sure, of course, as you are making the decision
to partner, that you are offering something unique and valuable.
In 1994, a Microsoft team worked with Julia Child to create a
beautiful CD-ROM of recipes and techniques. It looked like a

great team-up. However, the technology Microsoft offered was the same as other CD-ROM makers of the time. There was nothing special on the software front, and other cooking CD-ROMs were just as useful (although not quite as lovely).

It also turned out that electronic cookbooks didn't sell well. People thought about cooking mostly when they were in the kitchen and not when they were at their computer. Microsoft had neither the right technology nor the right customer offering to make the CD-ROM a success. While working with Julia Child was a pleasure and she gave the team a thrill whenever she'd call or visit, the CD-ROM failed to recover even the cost of creating it. In addition, Microsoft had signed a two CD-ROM contract with Julia Child. When the first one didn't sell well, Microsoft was still under contract to pay Julia for a second, even though that CD-ROM was never made.

KEEPING IT SIMPLE TAKES A LOT OF THOUGHT—THE MESSAGE IS THE MESSAGE

"When you tell someone the positioning of your product and they nod and say, 'Uh-huh,' as in, 'Well, of course,' you've just received one of the best compliments you'll get as a marketer." So says Jon Roberts, a general manager of Windows CE business development.

It's much harder to convince people to buy your product in thirty seconds than it is in thirty minutes. Unfortunately, you typically get the former instead of the latter. Nail a thirty-second version and you have the foundation for a clear, focused communication and marketing plan.

Remember, though, a simple, crisp message isn't always easy to create. It may take several rounds of brainstorming, customer feedback, experimentation, and a flop or two, to arrive at something that ends up sounding obvious. Also, it's useful to know how you're going to explain a new product before you start to build it.

Jon Roberts knows the value of keeping it simple. Over the past few years, his marketing teams have wrestled to create concise messages for Microsoft's complex operating systems. He found that the launch of Microsoft Windows version 3.0 epitomized the value of clear customer messages.

Microsoft Windows 3.0 product positioning revolved around the seemingly simple message "It's a whole new world." The marketing team thought this phrase captured the idea that this version of the product went way beyond what users had seen in the past.

The "new world" included a graphical (point and click) interface. For example a user could easily point and click on a button to open a spreadsheet instead of typing in a long string of commands. The same user could also run a word processor and a database at the same time! It's ancient history to us, but back in 1990, this was a radical new way to work on a PC. The changes to the program were extensive, and the marketing team found that it took quite a bit of explaining to convey all the changes.

The advertisements supporting the message consisted of an abstract image of a man leaping through a window. This symbolized leaping into a whole new world. The print told customers, "Kiss your DOS prompt good-bye." For those familiar with the product, this seemed like the perfect way to introduce customers to the exciting changes they were about to experience.

"Kiss my DOS prompt good-bye?" one customer moaned. "It's the only way I know to get this PC to work." Customers took one look at the ads and decided that they certainly didn't want to follow the man leaping through the window. No one knew what was on the other side. Besides, leaping through an open window just seemed like a bad idea. Instead of conveying excitement and innovation, the message simply promised radical change. The "benefits" of Windows were diverse, ranging from saving time to moving data easily, but there wasn't a unifying promise for the customer other than this radical change. And all that raised was concern.

Jon's team realized that this message wasn't the winner that they had proudly envisioned. They went back to their customers for more information. They heard a lot of different things, but the one predominant idea that came through time and time again was that customers just wanted the PC to be easier to use.

It was a valid point. The personal computer was not easy to use. And although the new version of Windows was still a complicated program for most customers, it did make the PC simpler. Such tasks as copying data from one program to another and finding files saved on the hard drive were much easier. Jon's team began to see "Windows makes the PC easy to use" as a possible way to position the diverse benefits of Windows 3.0.

"A whole new world," with its perceived threat of radical change, was out. Instead, the new Windows could offer a bridge between the old and difficult world of DOS and this new world of easier-to-use PCs. For customers, crossing a bridge seemed much easier and less risky than leaping out a window. "Windows makes PCs easier to use" became the new, simple, clear message. Advertisements, product demonstrations, marketing promotions, and all communication touted this single idea. The benefits that supported this message were folded into it. Compelling, and carrying a consumer benefit, this positioning was simple enough to be easily remembered by customers, but robust enough to hang a variety of features and promises from. The simple phrase became the solid foundation on which Jon's team built a successful marketing campaign.

Timing is key. In contrast to the above, "A whole new way to work" attracted, rather than frightened, customers of Office 4.0. The slogan and accompanying materials were all about making things consistent and easy. Those inconsistencies (different spell checkers in Word and PowerPoint, for example) had been infuriating. People eagerly embraced the new software. For the next version, though, the marketing team couldn't use that same slogan again. Users of Office had just changed to the last "whole new way to work" and they liked it. They weren't about to learn a whole other way to work!

Lessons I Learned about
Getting the Buzz Going on Your Product

Ben Waldman, General Manager, Macintosh Business Unit:

1. **Seed influential end users.**

   This one's a classic Microsoft strategy. Give your product away to opinion makers and trendsetters. Find customers who give their coworkers lots of advice in your product area. Find the customers who have purchasing power in the workplace. You want those folks to know your product, like it, and recommend it. Get it in their hands.

2. **"High profile" testimonials work for more than sneakers.**

   When Apple CEO Steve Jobs says he uses Microsoft Internet Explorer for the Macintosh, rather than Netscape's browser, it carries a lot of weight with Apple loyalists. The same is true when Guy Kawasaki, a well-known pundit in the Mac community, says he used Microsoft Word to write his latest book. It sounds geeky but that really matters.

3. **Show your product under NDA.**

   A nondisclosure agreement (NDA) means industry analysts, press people, and customers can take a look at your product but are prohibited from describing its features. This lets you show key contacts what you've got without letting the details slip to competitors (usually!). People under NDA can't say what you've got, but they *can* give their opinion as in, "I wish I could tell you what's in it...all I can say is you're going to love it." The suspense builds your cachet.

TO SHIP OR NOT TO SHIP...

Your team has worked hard on your new product. It looks like
it is ready, but you know that it's not quite perfect. Perhaps
the speed is a little too slow when compared to the competition or the quality of the packaging isn't what you had
expected. Maybe you are launching a new Web site, but it
could look snazzier or be easier to navigate. These aren't
"showstoppers," like a software bug that eats data or a toy
that injures kids. That would definitely put your product on
hold. Your situation is not as clear. You must decide if you
should ship now or wait until you get the final kinks out.

Your "new" product might be brand-new to the market or the
fifth update to an old favorite. Either way, putting a "not quite
ready for prime time" product out there can be a complete disaster or a brilliant marketing coup. Now is the time to step
back from the heat of your product development efforts and
take a close, unemotional look at the situation.

The obvious first question is "How bad are the problems?"
Keep in mind that if customers try your new product once and
it's not up to par, they may never give you another chance. So
ask the hard questions. What is the opportunity cost of holding
the product back? How much revenue will you lose? Will you
need extra resources and people to keep working? Will the team
have to put other work on hold to continue on this project?

Also, what are your competitors' plans? Are you racing
them to market? You may decide to send out something
slightly flawed just so the competition won't get the jump on
you. Are they already the market leader? In that case, waiting
until you can offer a superior product may be the way to go.

Leading an effort to create new software, Jeff Thiel, product
unit manager for Microsoft's Desktop Finance division, struggled with this dilemma. Jeff's goal was to get Microsoft into

the U.S. "consumer tax-preparation market." In other words, to get people to use their computers and Microsoft's new tax software to complete and file their tax returns. His team had pushed themselves for months to get the product completed for the 1999 tax season. In addition, Jeff had made several high-profile partnerships with other companies to help move the product along more quickly. Complicating the equation was that another company already had a product on the market. Missing the tax season would put Microsoft further behind.

Unlike other types of software, or most other products where feature trade-offs could be made, the tax team couldn't leave anything out of the product. The software had to include every major and every minor new tax change of the year. Also, other products have more flexibility as to when they reach the market. With tax software, if the team missed the January-to-April tax-preparation season, the sales for that year would be zero. And, much of the work they had put into changing the code for that tax year would be wasted because they would have to retool the product to reflect the changes in the tax code for the next tax season.

Work on the tax software progressed, but there were a lot of unknowns. The deadline was looking ugly. Jeff and his team were faced with the difficult task of deciding to ship or not. The question didn't seem straightforward.

REASONS TO HOLD BACK

Even a small glitch in the tax software could prove deadly. The calculation engine had to be perfect. Screwing up someone's tax return was more than undesirable: it could lead to a lawsuit. If the team pushed to get the product out, was there a chance that it could include a bug that could miscalculate taxes owed? And if even a minor mistake was made, would a customer lose faith in *all* the calculations? "I'd go recheck everything by hand if I found one mistake," one consumer said,

"and what would the use of the software be if I had to manu-
ally check everything?" Comments like that showed quality to
be a paramount need.

The tax team looked critically at all the features of the product. "Wizards" guided the customer, step-by-step, through filing
a 1040. It calculated everything from business expenses to mort-
gage interest to investment gains or losses to medical and child-
care exemptions. It was certainly a solid product, but not a slam
dunk over market leader, Intuit's Turbo Tax. If Jeff's team
waited a year, the team could add some key features that would
help Microsoft win product reviews and delight customers.

Jeff also looked at the monetary cost. What would a year's
extra work on the product cost and how much revenue would
they forgo in the year if they held it back?

REASONS TO GO AHEAD

Reasons to hold the product another year were mounting. But,
pressure escalated as well for the product to ship right away.
An estimated 1.5 million people per year were joining the
ranks of the electronic filers on an existing base of about 5.5
million. The market was taking off. Add the fact that each
buyer was likely to lend it to one friend to use, and the number
looked even more compelling. As more people used a PC to
calculate and submit tax returns, missing a year of sales meant
all new users would likely go with the market leader, Turbo
Tax. As Turbo Tax gained users, their market share could make
them the de facto standard, the "obvious" choice. This year's
sales could snowball into perpetuity.

Another factor was the energy level of the team. They had
agreed to an aggressive deadline from the get-go. They had
been pouring over their PCs well into the night, ordering take-
out dinners to eat in the communal conference room. Would
they have the stamina to put an entire additional year into the
product before they saw it shipped?

One last input was the possibility of "leaks." The longer the product was in production, the more time there was for information to slip out. In fact, Jeff confidentially told some software sellers what he thought Intuit's weaknesses were and how Microsoft's new product would address those. Lo and behold, the next announcement from Intuit detailed improvements for those exact areas. It could have been a coincidence, or a security breach.

THE DECISION

With all the pros and cons, the choice wasn't clear. Jeff went back to the fact that in this category he couldn't relax launch date, standards, or scope. It boiled down to a question of whether the team could get quality work done on time. The hard part was having to decide in August (when they needed to start making difficult-to-change commitments such as manufacturing capacity) if they'd be finished by November. How would Jeff know whether they could ship something they'd be proud of, in time to matter?

Jeff realized he couldn't assess the status of every piece of the puzzle. It really came down to the confidence of the team itself, so he put the decision into their hands. Jeff called a meeting of the managers who reported to him. He asked them to develop a set of objective criteria/metrics to meet by August that would give them a 95 percent confidence level of finishing in November. The criteria included completion of key product features, the fraction of the tax law changes implemented by that date, and product speed. Specific customer task scenarios had to be complete as well, including complicated returns with multiple financial ingredients such as Schedule C's and passive investments.

At the end of August the team had met a large number of the criteria, were close on some others, and had fallen significantly short on several important ones. In the end, the metrics that the team had developed and graded themselves on made the decision almost easy. The Microsoft tax software would wait a year.

Three Lessons I've Learned about Getting the New Product Out the Door

Chris Peters, Vice President, Interactive
Media Division:

1. **Find the force factor.**
   What's the one thing that's going to stop your product from succeeding? Identify it, watch it, buffer it, and make some contingency plans.
2. **Shipping is a feature.**
   Getting the product out on time is just as important as adding that last whizzy bell or whistle.
3. **Machiavelli says don't hire mercenaries to defend the castle. You might say the same goes for consultants.**
   They can be an extra resource, an objective opinion, or a brainstorming facilitator. But when it comes to working on the strategic lifeblood of your company, full-time employees have more of a stake in the project's success.

CHAPTER 4

Not-So-New
Products

Your product or service is in the marketplace. In fact it has been for some time. How do you keep it fresh in the minds of your customers? When is it time to improve your product? Are you even really sure who your competitors are?

This period, "sustaining" marketing, as it is known at Microsoft, uses some of the same tactics and strategies as new product or "launch" marketing. Certainly both require creativity, planning, and skillful execution. Both types of marketing teams need to think about meeting customer needs, fending off competitors, and setting up their teams to respond to opportunities and dangers.

The difference is the time pressure. Launching a new product is a stressful confluence of myriad efforts. The product has to be fully tested in time to meet its manufacturing schedule. Salespeople and international subsidiaries need to be trained when they receive samples. Advertisements need to be created and placed in the time leading up to the product's delivery to stores. The press release must be transmitted over the wire on the day customers can make the first purchase.

With sustaining marketing (i.e., your product has been launched, and now you need to sustain interest and sales) there should be time to sit back and survey. There may be surprises that require quick action, but now is your chance to reanalyze the market. Make sure your sales force or dealer network is well equipped to sell. Review your product's importance to customers, think about possible improvements, and clean up any mess you made when the product was introduced (for example, smudged relationships and broken promises). You can also take stock of any negative perceptions or perceived weaknesses and set them right.

MOMENTUM RELEASES AND OTHER TRICKS TO KEEP YOUR PRODUCT IN THE NEWS

When Microsoft launches a new product into the market, a press release is sent over the newswire, filled with product benefits, glowing quotes from users or distributors, and other fabulous information that the Microsoft team hopes will end up in print.

Last year Microsoft sent out hundreds of press releases, but didn't ship hundreds of new products. Still, these press releases were full of product benefits, great quotes, and other fabulous information. And again Microsoft hoped these releases would be picked up by journalists and printed. If the products weren't new, what was all the hoopla about? What other kind of "news" warranted a press release?

A consummate skill of the Microsoft PR machine is keeping Microsoft products in the news. This PR coverage translates to free advertising; a reporter is telling readers about your products, and you're not paying him or her to do it. The ideas and tactics Microsoft uses can be applied to products and services across any industry. Just give the press corps positive, accurate, and most importantly, *compelling* information to see your product's name in print. Three ways Microsoft does this is a press buddy system, rapid response teams, and momentum press releases.

PRESS BUDDIES

Microsoft executives and managers form ongoing relationships with press people. They may send a weekly E-mail update, call once a month on the phone, or initiate whatever level of contact is felt the press person would like to have. Over time, the reason for the call or E-mail doesn't have to be a piece of news or a story to pitch. The Microsoftie will just call to say hello, chat, and keep the reporter up-to-date on the latest happenings at the company. These calls are relationship builders, rather than story-makers.

As long as you don't end up bothering or badgering the reporter, these relationships can be worthwhile for both sides. The influential press people will always be on top of your products, strategies, and industry. If they have a personal relationship with you, they may go to you first to get an opinion or information, rather than your competitor. They're more likely to call you, a reliable contact, when they are on a short deadline. And as in the case of a software bug in Microsoft Word a few years ago, they may even call and give you a chance to defend yourself before printing a negative article.

Other companies use the same strategy, trying to cultivate even higher levels. Microsoft competitors Marc Andreessen, of Netscape, and Kim Polese, of Marimba software, are said to be tight with U.S. Vice President Al Gore, meeting with him to discuss software policy issues and technology.

RAPID RESPONSE TEAMS

Rapid response teams don't just sit around waiting for something to respond to. In fact, there really is no "rapid response team" at Microsoft. The rapid responders are just the people doing the everyday marketing jobs at Microsoft. When a crisis or opportunity hits, they briefly become the rapid response team, jumping to do damage control or to make the most of a situation, and then returning to their normal life.

Here are a few examples of Microsoft's rapid response mentality:

The Expedia travel service likes to be ahead of its competitors and likes everyone else to know it too. So their typical rapid response focuses on a competitor's action. When its rivals send out a press release touting great sales, numbers of users, or other good news, Expedia tries to trump them by whipping out its own press release with even more impressive numbers. The opposing data from Expedia keeps journalists aware of Expedia's position in the marketplace. If a story comes out based on the competitor's press release, it will probably include Expedia's positive numbers too.

The America Online–Sun Microsystems–Netscape alliance at the end of 1998 set off wild speculation among journalists. Who were the players now? What would the implications be for Microsoft? The Microsoft Network started receiving calls for their reaction. Susan Weeber, PR manager for the Microsoft Network, wanted to show Microsoft's position vis-à-vis the new competitive landscape. The PR team took the calls but also wanted to broadcast Microsoft's strengths more widely. Susan created a press release listing powerful partner-ships, commerce expansion, and evidence that Microsoft's growth was outpacing that of America Online and Yahoo. This way, she delivered accurate, positive information on the situation, to customers, press, and industry partners.

Sometimes, the rapid response is meant to keep your product *out* of the news, rather than in it. Within the first week of Windows 95 hitting the market, a rumor surfaced in Spain that one of the product's disks carried a computer virus. Interestingly, the rumor was tracked back to a company that made antivirus software. The Microsoft team quickly examined the situation and determined that the disk didn't contain a virus, but did expose a certain virus if it existed on a computer already.

For the computer geeks among you, here are the details: Floppy disk number two of the Windows installation disks used a new compression technology that "write protected" its boot sector. The virus that already existed on some machines would copy itself onto any floppy's boot sector. Because the Windows disk's boot sector was protected, the virus wouldn't copy onto it and the PC wouldn't read the disk. Users thought the disk itself was bad when their PC wouldn't read it.

The Microsoft PR team quickly informed all key news outlets of the real situation before those newspeople heard it as a rumor from somewhere else. The Microsoft product team sent out that same information to business partners and Microsoft managers around the world so they wouldn't get embroiled in the situation. As a result, only few articles were written, and the rumor didn't run rampant.

MOMENTUM PRESS RELEASES

Momentum releases are one of my favorite PR tactics, tantamount to creating news when there is none. Sending out a press release with any type of "first," "best," "award," or "weird thing" for your product is likely to get picked up, read, and reprinted in a magazine or newspaper. It may even garner you a TV or radio interview. Examples of this PR tactic are everywhere. A recent blurb in the *New York Times* touted an ATM machine at the top of the World Trade Center in New York as the world's highest cash machine. Is that really news? No, but it got publicity for the bank and the ATM machine.

The usual reason to write a momentum release is to get back in the public eye. To do this, you first need to appear on the press's radar. Supply them with fascinating information about your company's growth, product improvements, key hires—i.e., your momentum. Do you have a millionth customer? Are you filing lots of patents? Get them to think about writing a story about you, or using your information in a broader story they're working on.

Consolidating minor news events is another excuse to put together a momentum release. Each tidbit may not be worthy of its own story, but together, they pack a punch. Microsoft does this with industry partners, groups of small business deals, even numbers of advertisers who have decided to post ads on the Microsoft Network, to show that property's growing popularity.

Some Microsoft products make ongoing momentum releases part of their marketing plan, right from the start. "Rolling Thunder," an expression coined during the Windows 3.1 launch, included a series of planned press releases. Software makers, computer manufacturers, corporate customers, and retailers each had a press release focused on their adoption and excitement surrounding Windows 3.1. An Egghead Software store manager might be quoted saying, "We can't keep it on the shelves." A corporate customer would say, "We plan to deploy this to twenty thousand desktops within one year." Rolling Thunder included internal PR as well, rallying the whole company behind the product. Flashy demos and in-depth technical talks psyched up everyone from secretaries to programmers. At the national sales meeting, the sales force was inundated with pep talks, selling strategies, and tchotchkes imprinted with the Windows logo.

Three Important Definitions
Author Unknown

1. **Ohnosecond:**
   That minuscule fraction of time in which you realize that you've just made a BIG mistake.
2. **Percussive Maintenance:**
   The fine art of whacking the c**p out of an electronic device to get it to work again.
3. **Adminisphere:**
   The rarefied organizational layers beginning just above the rank and file. Decisions that fall from the adminisphere are often profoundly inappropriate or irrelevant to the problems they were designed to solve.

RIDE SOMEONE'S COATTAILS TO GET THE MOST OUT OF A SMALL BUDGET

Despite their propensity to think big, Microsoft managers sometimes do start small. Sure the executives hope every new venture will grow into a widely popular, wildly profitable product, but they don't pour funding into every idea. Yes, the company could probably buy itself into any market segment, but that wouldn't really show if the product could stand on its own or at least generate more revenue than expenses.

The venture has to prove itself before it is assigned significant promotional funds. So, a Microsoft product may start out with a tiny marketing budget. It's up to that team to be creative with its resources and get a jump start on the road to success.

In 1996, Microsoft created an on-line travel magazine called *Mungo Park* after the famed eighteenth-century Scottish explorer. *Mungo Park,* the magazine, would send popular writers and personalities on expeditions to unexpected places around the globe. The adventurers would then send back word, video, and photos of their experiences, sometimes via satellite, and *Mungo Park* readers would enjoy the trip vicariously.

The team had few marketing dollars to spend, but wanted exposure and awareness for the magazine. To get more bang for their bucks, they teamed up with some bigger names and media properties and created events. Lyle Lovett motorcycled through Chile, Shari Belafonte trekked through Costa Rica. One *Mungo Park* team-up sent Dr. Ruth Westheimer to the Trobriands, Papua New Guinea's "Islands of Love," and broadcast the first 360-degree photograph from the Trobriands ever to appear on the World Wide Web. Sex expert Dr. Ruth wrote of the sexual rituals and habits of the people there.

Another *Mungo Park* adventure brought Martha Stewart to Newfoundland to explore the country and examine boat-making. Martha tied the subject matter back to her television show, so her efforts and *Mungo Park*'s referenced each other, sending the viewers of each to the other's media property.

On a "you'll never know where you'll end up" side note... Mark Kroese, the general manager of Microsoft's *Mungo Park,* worked with Martha Stewart in Newfoundland. Later, he left the company to write a book about favorite climbs of famous mountain climbers. He received a call from Martha Stewart's office inviting him to be the "technology guy" on her show, explaining things like the Internet. Now you'll see him on TV. Go figure.

Mungo Park's next team-up was with NASA—yes, the U.S. space program. Microsoft worked with astronaut John Grunsfeld to deliver the first live dispatches to a Web site from space. When I asked Janet Angell, the marketer for *Mungo Park,* how she persuaded NASA to work with her webzine, she replied, "We did our homework on the organization to see what might be a win-win promotion with them and offered a prepackaged idea. It was great PR for *Mungo Park* to have an astronaut interacting with our readers, and we had a magazine that met NASA's standards for editorial integrity." The NASA connection brought lots of new users to the *Mungo Park* Web site, and garnered millions of dollars of free PR coverage, but still, too few advertisers were buying space on *Mungo Park.* The site wasn't paying for itself. They needed a new strategy.

The next coattails *Mungo Park* tried to ride were those of Expedia, the on-line travel service. *Mungo Park* changed their content and approach a bit to become a "feeder" to the travel agency, sending readers there to book travel. They hoped to keep a percentage of whatever Expedia made. But this didn't generate enough revenue to sustain them either. Eventually, the magazine folded.

Now you may be thinking, "If all this riding someone else's

coattails failed, why are you recommending it to us?" This particular venture did fail, but the idea makes sense. The increase in users and PR exposure was great for *Mungo Park;* it just wasn't enough in the early days of the Web when advertisers were scarce and paying magazine subscribers even scarcer. Microsoft continues to use other media properties, personalities, or events to boost their marketing dollars.

One last caveat is to make sure that the coattails you're riding on make sense to your target audience. Microsoft's "Bob" software helped people organize and manage their households. The Bob team hired Shelley Long (*Cheers* actress) to pitch "getting organized" with a newsletter, how-to tips, refrigerator magnets, the works. The PR group who pitched this idea assured the Bob team of great coverage and they delivered. Shelley and her message appeared on newscasts, on morning talk shows, and in magazine articles.

Listeners, however, paid no attention. They didn't order the free "get organized with Microsoft Bob" kits that Shelley was offering. Yes, they thought of themselves as busy. Yes, they thought of themselves as juggling lots of tasks and responsibilities. But few wanted to think of themselves as *un*organized. Few would admit it. The PR coverage was fabulous, but any follow-through to sales flopped entirely. The idea was perfectly packaged to be promoted, but not to be successful!

Three Lessons I've Learned about Making Decisions

Dean Hachamovitch, Group Program Manager,
Microsoft Office Group:

1. **If you set priorities for your project, there will be "musts" and "likes."**
   Accept that "likes" might not happen. Your responsibility as a manager is to make sure the "musts" do.
2. **How do you choose between different "musts?" Magic bullets.**
   Think about having one magic bullet that can do anything—what would you spend it on? Use the hard prioritization of the magic-bullet exercise to resolve deadlocks over scarce resources.
3. **Be willing to make a decision.**
   I once interviewed someone who could see both sides of every position but wouldn't make a decision—even when I asked him what kind of bag I should choose when buying groceries. I didn't hire him. If you spend all your time contemplating or revisiting decisions, there's no time left to execute them.

CREATE A SHADOW COMPETITION

Your competition may or may not be scary right now. But there's always the looming specter that someone is poised to do something big in your marketspace. Creating your own "shadow competition" will better prepare you for the unexpected onslaught, slick move, or market shift. This knowledge may direct you to add the equivalent of a car's cup-holder to your product or to try to put it on a whole new growth curve.

In 1996, some people wondered if Dennis Tevlin, director of marketing for Microsoft Office software, actually had anything to do. After all, Microsoft's word-processing and spreadsheet software enjoyed 80–90 percent market share in the category. Lotus and WordPerfect were no longer threats to the Office business. So, what did Dennis do every day—other than avoid screwing up the business? And what did his large marketing team do? Sit around and count the money they were making?

To keep the troops on their toes, Dennis led an exercise called "creating the shadow competition." The team picked apart the competition's strengths and weaknesses and then turned their critical eye on themselves. The outcome? They created "the perfect competitor," a fictional but potential presence that could storm the market.

To concoct this flawless nemesis, Dennis's group discussed direct competitors to word-processing software and spreadsheets, as well as competitors outside this narrow band. They stretched the meaning of "competition" to include a variety of things competing for their customers' time and dollars. They looked beyond their existing definition of the market and examined potential and current trends.

Dennis and his team concluded that rather than looking at their share of dollars of the office software market, they should broaden their focus to the overall computer desktop. And rather than money, they looked at time as the measure of value. On a typical computer on someone's desk at work, what was Microsoft software's share in time spent? Time spent could equate to the value that software held for the company. The more time spent using that tool, the more critical it might be to the performance of the company.

One trend that was immediately obvious in 1996 was the increase of E-mail use in the workplace. As more businesses adopted E-mail, as it started to replace phone answering machines, as people's electronic in-boxes began filling more and more each day, E-mail was becoming critical to doing business. The Microsoft Office software box had always included a license that entitled the user to use Microsoft E-mail but not the software. The company's network administrator had to install the E-mail software from a central location.

The team worked with the product designers and developers to include the E-mail software itself in the Office box, allowing users to install it as part of their basic Office installation. This was not a move the team might have made if they had just looked at the traditional Office market. The move helped Microsoft's E-mail market share explode.

Another change the team noticed was *how* people were using Office software. Office was originally designed for the solitary worker. Typical users would author a memo or create a budget spreadsheet by themselves. After research with the product designers and some customers, Dennis and his team learned that office workers were collaborating more and sharing information. They coauthored reports and had multiple groups building financial spreadsheets.

To increase the value of Office and to increase the time people spent with it, the team added "workgroup" features. Now people could work together more easily because Office let them readily comment on each other's work, assemble various parts into one document, and then send it around for review. Again, if the team had limited themselves to looking at their product's value in dollars instead of time, they would not have considered this new and lucrative way to market the product.

By expanding its notion of competition beyond the norm, Microsoft Office avoided sitting placidly on its dominant market share and continued improving its product.

WHO IS YOUR COMPETITOR?

According to management guru Michael Porter, "Strategic groups may face differing levels of exposure to competition from substitute products if they are focusing on different parts of the product line, serving different customers, operating at different levels of quality or technological sophistication, have different cost positions, and so on."* Sometimes the elements above can create surprising competitors. Based on certain factors, you may think you are competing with a set of products or services, then find out otherwise.

Microsoft Works for the Macintosh is a software suite that features a slimmed-down word processor and spreadsheet. It is less sophisticated and priced lower than Microsoft Office, Microsoft's bigger and more complex software suite. Although Office had a very complete and sophisticated set of features, in the early 1990's it was also expensive and required a great deal of disk space. Works was developed for home and small-business users who didn't need the power and price associated with Office. As Works manager Linda Mitchell wrote her marketing plan, she saw her competition as Claris Works, a similar product in size, cost, and feature set. She developed a positioning statement that differentiated her product from Claris Works. She measured her value proposition against theirs. She compared her technological features to theirs.

Luckily, before she implemented her plans, she carefully researched her potential customer base—home and small-business users. To her surprise, she found more of them owned Microsoft Office, the full-blown software suite, than owned Claris Works. The choice factors she thought were relevant— price and disk space—were not the important ones. Customers

---

*Michael Porter, *Competitive Strategy*, p. 137.

were willing to pay more and give up disk space to get the additional features. Her main competition was her *own* company.

As strange as it seems, it's not that unusual to compete with yourself. Procter and Gamble has more than one laundry detergent, and PepsiCo certainly owns more than one fast-food chain. Even a small company, such as a local family-owned ice-cream maker, might be competing with its own flavors rather than the competitor's line.

In another twist, you may find you are competing with a set of totally different products. A friend in business school recounted the day at Kraft when her Velveeta teammate declared, "I thought we were leading the 'loaf cheese' market, but it turns out there is no 'loaf cheese' market!" So don't assume you know which products your customers are choosing between until you find some data to prove it.

YOUR WORST CRITICS CAN TURN INTO YOUR BIGGEST ADVOCATES

A lesson taught in college Psychology 101 goes something like this. If someone starts out disliking you and then ends up liking you, they will often like you more than the person who has liked you all along. I'm sure that's a vast simplification that will make Cornell professor James Maas cringe, but that's the gist of it. The same can be true in business. A vicious rival can turn that competitive energy into a strong alliance. Upset customers can sometimes turn around to become your biggest fans.

Ben Waldman, general manager of the Macintosh Business Unit at Microsoft, has lived through this lesson. It started out quite ugly. Customers completely and utterly hated Microsoft's Word 6.0 for the Macintosh when it was launched in 1995. They deemed it "slow, buggy, and not at all Mac-like." To them, it capped off an inexorable degradation of Microsoft's Macintosh software quality and was empty lip service to "Apple customer commitment." At the 1995 Mac World computer trade show, Microsoft employees got booed and yelled at. Nasty product reviews appeared in the press such as the one with the headline "Word 6-0h My God!" Web sites appeared dedicated to excoriating Microsoft. Bill Gates sent an E-mail saying he'd gotten more hate mail on the topic of Mac Word 6.0 than any other topic to date.

Microsoft thought it had been doing the right thing by making the Mac and Windows versions of its word processors look alike. After all, in corporations, there was a mix of Macintoshes and Windows PCs. Wouldn't it be a benefit for customers switching between machines for the software to look and act alike everywhere? Apparently not. Mac users wanted their software to look like Mac software and not like some poor cousin to Windows. They also felt the quality of the Mac software had been compromised to get the two to look alike (hence the "slow" and "buggy" epithets).

The Microsoft executives knew the situation was a disaster. And as with many business disasters, a small, autonomous group would offer the best solution. The executives created a separate Macintosh Business Unit, gave it the funds and decision-making power to turn the product around, and found a zealot (Ben) to lead it.

Ben Waldman knew he had to fix the Macintosh software products, change customer perception, and get the press on his side. Three tall orders when all three were in terrible shape. First he addressed the software itself. His team set out to identify the unique needs of the Mac customer. In the past, the Mac customer had been lumped in with all Office software users. In a survey of one hundred buyers, the requests of the handful of Mac users had been drowned out. Now, they'd have their own survey and more impact.

Besides fixing the obvious shortcomings, Ben's team invented new features and introduced them onto the Mac product before they appeared on the Windows version. This was a huge deal psychologically to the Mac customers, who were tired of seeing innovations on the Windows software and waiting six to twelve months to get in on the Mac (if ever). These new features ranged from just "kind of cool" to big time-savers. A couple of new capabilities earned the Mac team a thank-you from the U.S. space agency, NASA, who claimed they had saved one and a half hours per Mac per year in technician time.

There were enhancements for all kinds of Mac users. A click of the mouse on a word would display a little box listing synonyms—a great boon to writers. For those who complained the product wasn't "Mac-like," Ben and his team changed five hundred "dialogue boxes" in the software to the correct shade of Macintosh gray and put the "OK" button on the right, where Mac users were used to seeing it, instead of the left.

Ben started communicating more with Apple corporate executives, telling them what he and his team were planning. When he actually started to deliver on his promise of product improvements, they responded with enthusiasm. CEO Steve Jobs was so impressed when Ben showed him Microsoft's new Office 98 software that he invited Ben to join him onstage at the Mac World trade-show keynote address.

When Ben showed up onstage at Mac World, he was greeted by shocked hisses and grumbling from the audience. As he started showing the product's improvements, though, the crowd actually started cheering. The *San Jose Mercury News* reported that Ben received more applause than Steve Jobs. Now that Ben has shared the stage for keynote addresses with Steve Jobs, from Paris to New York to Tokyo, Mac customers are no longer surprised to see Microsoft and Apple together. Those joint appearances do more to improve customer perception of Microsoft's Macintosh commitment than a host of ads could.

Following the successful Office software launch, Ben and his teamed focused on their Internet browser. Rather than waiting for the new Windows version of Internet Explorer to come out, Ben went out on his own, fixing problems in the product and again introducing new features on the Macintosh platform before they came out on the Windows product. When it became available, more people downloaded Internet Explorer 4.5 Macintosh Edition in its first two weeks than had ever downloaded the previous version.

Along with the product developments came marketing. Ben met with the press, giving them sneak previews, talking up Microsoft's commitment to turning the situation around, and proving it with product enhancements. As a result, even the writer who came out with the "Word 6-0h My God!" article now has a friendly relationship with Ben and has written glowing articles. That same journalist, David Pogue, penned an article saying he had to see his therapist. The reason? He wanted so badly to hate Microsoft but their new Macintosh products were so good! Another former Microsoft excoriator, Guy Kawasaki, wrote his latest book using Microsoft Word.

At the beginning of his tenure as general manager on the Mac business, Ben told his team, "We'll know we've been successful when a Mac user at a trade show wants to buy you a drink or give you a hug, instead of yell at you." His team thought he was utterly nuts. In the end, though, it actually happened. "Apple users are fervent," says Ben. "They either really despise you or completely love you. It's much nicer to get on their good side." Apple's CEO, Steve Jobs, recently called Ben Waldman "one of the most passionate Mac advocates on the planet." Until recently, no one in the Mac community would have believed such a person could exist at Microsoft. Now actually, they do.

A DEFENSE SO STRONG
IT BECOMES AN OFFENSE

"Accept criticism. There's usually something, a kernel of truth in it, that will resonate with you." So says Dennis Tevlin, former director of marketing for the Desktop Applications Division. Put your bruised ego aside to find the truth in the criticism and then do something with it. You might find that your weak spot can become a strength.

In 1996, Sun, Oracle, and others were touting the new network computer (NC) and its advantages over the standard PC that everyone had on his or her desk. They talked about how expensive a PC was for training, software, and network management. They argued that the NC could greatly decrease these costs.

The NC advocates had convincing arguments. Companies could use these machines with lower memory, slower CPUs, and smaller hard disks (or none at all), to reduce costs on new machines purchased and/or extend the life of older machines. Also, the standard PC stored copies of software it used on its hard disk. In contrast, the NC could store the software centrally. Like a library, the NC could check out copies to users as they needed them. Companies could own fewer copies of the software (save money) and free up disk space on their desktop computers. Storing software centrally was also more convenient for the people running the corporate computers. Software updates would be made to a few tightly controlled central computers instead of everyone's machine separately. This made the NC vastly appealing to technology managers. Corporate modifications, such as special menu items or subprograms, could be created once and stored centrally as well, rather than modifying every user's machines.

This centralization would save time and money, but there were drawbacks. Users lost flexibility. It was more difficult to personalize their software for their specific tasks. Also, common duties, such as word processing, took longer because NC performance from a central location, was slower. The data had to go back and forth across the wires of the network, rather than just operating on the PC on a person's desk. Many usage scenarios (such as bringing your laptop home at night or on the airplane) would be impossible if a corporate connection was required. Users even lost some control of their data, since it was stored at one main site. This was somewhat antithetical to the "personal" nature of personal computing, which many users saw as a step backward.

Despite its drawbacks, businesses eagerly responded to the promise of the NC's easy rollout and maintenance. The NC was a big threat to Microsoft's bread-and-butter software, Office. To respond, the Office team undertook the mission to match and even surpass the abilities of the NC. It would have been easy to dismiss this trend on the basis of the shortcomings mentioned above. Microsoft didn't think that users would give up control of their documents (local storage), that network performance would be fast enough for all users, or that the laptop usage scenarios (which were gaining momentum) would be possible. The press was also getting in on the action, creating a showdown scenario between NC advocates and Microsoft—always good for circulation. So many opinions were flying around that customers had a hard time separating fact from fiction.

Microsoft needed to look carefully and objectively at the NC's value, rather than give a knee-jerk "our way is the best way." Microsoft needed to extract the good parts of the NC vision, such as lowering costs, allowing more central management of software, and making computing simpler for the average user. The Microsoft team didn't want to eliminate, however, what they considered to be the best parts of their current offering to achieve this. They challenged themselves to combine the best of personal computing with the best of network computing and deliver a better solution to the customer. They tried not to get embroiled in the press frenzy, but seriously considered the criticisms leveled against them.

The Office team redesigned their software to offer the benefits of both the NC and the PC. For companies and customers who wanted things done centrally, they made Office operable from one main spot. For users who wanted the software customized for them, Microsoft continued enhancing those features in the products. They figured flexibility to go either way was better than just matching the centralization capabilities of the NC. Rather than go to parity, they went beyond it to regain their competitive advantage. Many other factors kept the NC out of the mainstream (for example, it couldn't run the most popular software), but changes in Microsoft's Office software, and similar improvements in Microsoft Windows, to give customers the best of both worlds, were also responsible.

JUST BECAUSE CUSTOMERS DIDN'T ASK FOR IT DOESN'T MEAN THEY DON'T WANT IT

It's great to get customer feedback and then include their wishes in your product or service. But customers can't always anticipate what they'll need. They don't always know what the latest technology or manufacturing techniques may mean for them. Sometimes they don't mention something because they assume it won't change. You're the ultimate expert on what can and can't change in your product or service. Ask customers' opinions but temper their feedback with feasibility. Then, think about the questions that you didn't ask them before you make your product plans.

To upgrade Microsoft Office—the suite of products including a spreadsheet, word processor, and other work-related software—the design team of 1994 hit the pavement. They visited corporate customers around the world to ask how they used their computers, why, when, where, and for what. They watched people using Microsoft's current software and counted every keystroke. They tallied up all the calls to the Microsoft product support line and categorized them by problem area. From this exhaustive research (well, *they* really were exhausted, anyway), the team compiled a list of the customers' favorite features, the things that drove them nuts, the parts of the software they never used, and new capabilities they wanted to see added.

The resulting release, Office 4.0, had some nice new features. It even provided more consistency in the look and feel between the word processor and the spreadsheet. It was a solid upgrade... but users *freaked out!*

Any memo, spreadsheet, report, or anything created using the previous version of Office couldn't be loaded, viewed, or worked on in the new version. Any new work created using Office 4.0 couldn't be read, used, or edited by the previous version. Microsoft, working to improve the fundamental performance of the software, had changed the underlying file format. Microsoft included a file converter, but it was a pain in the neck to use. This all came as quite a shock since a new file format hadn't been mentioned in customer feedback.

Corporations *hated* the change in file format. With hundreds or thousands of users, they weren't planning on switching everyone to the new software overnight. They were going to phase in the new version of Office gradually. With the new file format, people using the new version would not be able to share documents with people using the old version. Imagine trying to roll up budgets, build project plans, or just create a simple presentation if more than one person or even department were trying to work together. With a slow, phased-in roll out to thousands of users in a corporation, conflicts constantly arose over who was using which software version and who could or could not share their work.

The Microsoft design team thought they had been listening to customers by asking them what they wanted. But no customer said, "Oh, by the way, don't change the file format." They didn't mention it because they assumed it wasn't going to change. And no one at Microsoft asked, "Oh, by the way, can we change the file format?"

Customers created such a stink over this unanticipated change that Microsoft tried not to change the Office file format again unless the reasons for the change (such as enabling Internet access and publishing) were compelling. And this time, the team told customers *in advance* that the file format was changing. They also gave customers tools to ease the transition such as "readers," which let people view any Word file, no matter its format. The team learned that customer feedback wasn't a panacea for perfect product design, but was just one step in the process.

Three Lessons I've Learned about Invigorating the Troops

Jeff Raikes, Group Vice President:

1. **Wrap a fun theme around the serious goals.**
   One year, dressed as a Guardian Angel in white T-shirt and red beret, I performed a rap song for thousands of salespeople. I wasn't sure of the impact until I met later that year with the Chicago sales team at their office. I showed up and they were all wearing white T-shirts and red berets. Each annual theme rallies the sales organization around our key business objectives in a festive way for the whole year.

2. **Expose employees to senior executives.**
   During the last yearly review, Steve (Ballmer, Microsoft president) and I noticed that our revenue as a percentage of our competitor Novell's Netware sales was much lower in Poland than in the Czech Republic. The Polish managers weren't sure why. We helped them break down their data into smaller categories to find where the weakness lay. During that same review period, Steve spent nearly thirty minutes challenging the Greek subsidiary's request to hire one additional person. He wants to teach each general manager to take every headcount decision seriously. Personal interaction with senior execs often gets managers energized as we think through their business together.

3. **Send strong signals via a meeting's agenda.**
   This year, Steve Ballmer asked the foreign-subsidiary managers to put their top three employee concerns on the first page of their annual state-of-the-business presentation. Putting this item at the top of the agenda, before even the year's sales results, and allowing plenty of time for discussion, showed the importance Steve was placing on keeping and developing great people.

DON'T FIX IT, FEATURE IT

Often customer complaints will make you think, "Yeah, we should change that." However, the changes you make may not make everyone happy. The press might bad-mouth your strategy. Customers might gripe about a decision into which you put a lot of time. Or, a competitor now sees an opportunity to put your product down. Don't panic. Figure out another way to position your product, service, or strategy to win the outside world back to your camp.

Bloatware! This is what software-industry press people loved to call Microsoft Office. They argued Office took up way too much computer hard disk space because the design team kept cramming more and more features into the product. They argued that Microsoft was adding new capabilities, one on top of another, just to make people feel they had to buy the next new version. These industry pundits cried that the new features were too esoteric or just a plain waste of time.

The term *bloatware* spread quickly. When Microsoft salespeople visited large-customer accounts, they were continually asked why Office was so big. Echoing the press, technology managers complained, "The average person only uses twenty percent of the product. What do we need the rest of it for? It just slows everything down." It sounded as if the product had to be cut severely or Microsoft Office would start losing major sales. Then again, maybe it was just the product's perception that needed changing.

The Office team kicked into high gear to combat the bloatware image. They agreed that most people used only 20 percent of the software's capabilities—but each person's 20 percent could be completely different. One person might use the desktop publishing features to make coupons and flyers. Another person might use only the mail merge and envelope features. Yet another person might spend most of his time with the redlining and annotating features. The Office team contended that having all these features in one product provided more flexibility for their customers. And in a world where job and department changes are common, a flexible product could meet the customer's needs without forcing the customer to learn a new product. So if a small-business owner decided that in addition to producing her own flyers, she also wanted to mail them, she just learned a few more features in Office instead of learning a completely different software program. But putting a new spin on the product would not entirely quell the rising mutiny.

The press had complained that new capabilities were added just to make people buy a new product. The truth was that the customers themselves had mostly requested those new features. Still, if no one seemed to be using the enhancements, it was easy to criticize them. The Microsoft team wanted people to be able to find and use all the product's features. They also realized folks were not going to read a manual or go to a training class—few had the time or patience. Still, the team had put all those new features in the product for a reason; the problem was how to make them accessible. The answer came in the form of a "training wizard," which provided assistance on the appropriate topic at the appropriate time. If the software sensed you were trying to accomplish a task, it would offer help. For example, if you typed "Dear Aidan," Office would assume you were writing a letter and offer help in formatting it. Or, you could go to the Help feature and, in plain English, type a question like "How do I make mailing labels?" and the instructions for that function would appear.

The Office team had a broad set of features to offer and wanted them available to the users on demand. So rather than caving in to complaints of "bloatware" and too many features, the Office team decided, "We won't fix it, we'll feature it." They explained why the variety of features was critical to customers and then made those capabilities easier to find and use. The situation has improved, but it hasn't completely played out. Small word-processing and other business software programs written in the Java programming language are nipping at Microsoft's heels. These programs tout their tiny size and nimbleness. So far, they haven't made major inroads into the corporate market because they lack many capabilities, but they keep the Microsoft team nervous and busy.

Three Lessons I've Learned about Getting the Most Out of Older Products

Robbie Bach, Vice President,
Home and Retail Products:

1. **You won't get the most out of an older product by "milking" it.**
   You need to keep investing via one or more of the following:
   - Marketing activities such as ads, promotions, and public relations
   - Product improvements
   - Line extensions
   - Add-on products/accessories
   - Subscriptions
2. **Create a "classics" line.**
   Scale down the packaging, bundle some older products together, and look for discount distribution opportunities such as warehouse stores.
3. **Extract every dollar from an asset by slowly lowering its price over time.**
   Early adopters pay more. Others who aren't as excited to buy your product will wait and pay less. For example, a game might need a price drop every holiday season.

SHUT DOWN AND SALVAGE

At Microsoft, as with other companies, it is harder to shut down an unprofitable area than it is to improve one that's already profitable. However, both actions help the company's bottom line. The trick is to salvage anything you can from the business you are shutting down—including ideas, processes, and if you can, the morale of the team working on it.

Microsoft "Bob," before it even hit the market, was the darling of the popular press. Product demonstrations made news with CNN, the *Wall Street Journal,* and other national media. "Finally, software my mother can use" was the buzz on the street.

Okay...maybe you've never heard of this cool product or don't remember seeing it. Microsoft Bob was a set of software products that were targeted at the home PC user market. Modules included an address book, list manager, calendar, and little animated helpers—thus the name Bob—who would guide users on how to use the modules. The Bob team was ecstatic with their cutting-edge concept and technology.

But Bob didn't turn out quite as expected. The product was delayed a number of times—years actually. When it finally hit the market, the technology had moved past it. But even more problematic was Bob himself. The little animated characters were a great idea to guide people through a step-by-step process such as making a grocery list or adding birthdays to a calendar. The characters even were helpful the second or third time someone did the same task. But by the tenth time through a task, people knew the steps and there was no shortcut. They got frustrated with the little dog or paper clip or talking whatever telling them how to get things done. Customers stopped using the product and did not recommend it to their friends. Sales stalled. Store shelves bulged with inventory. Cute, helpful Bob became a pariah.

The team was demoralized, having worked for years on a breakthrough idea that had flopped. Bob was failing and there was no way to fix him. His time had passed with the advent of new technology, and the fixes needed to appease customers were too costly and timely.

Team members didn't want their work to be in vain. After all, it had been born of countless hours of user research. The essence of Bob held something valuable, even if the team had to ditch the current execution. What could they salvage?

People did respond to Bob's animated assistants. This "social interface" made people comfortable communicating with the computer because the interaction seemed to come not from the computer but from an anthropomorphized character. The Office team saw that they could use the social interface. Word and Excel used them to guide people through new tasks they were learning on the software. This time, though, they could be used as an alternative way to guide users through a process or help them with a question. Users could then determine their own way to work, alleviating the biggest complaint about Bob.

The Bob team would have preferred that their original incarnation had succeeded. However, when it was clear that it would not, most of the team took some comfort in that their ideas lived on in other products at the company.

CHAPTER 5

The Partners You May
Not Think of as Partners
(Coworkers, Service Agencies,
Dealers, the Press)

A partner isn't just the person who has invested in your company in exchange for a percentage of its ownership. A partner isn't just the businessperson with a complementary product who goes on joint sales calls with you. The people you think of as "partner" should encompass anyone you're working with toward a common goal. Your boss and your coworkers should all be partners, because you share the same objectives (usually). Your ad agency is a partner; you both want well-placed, effective advertising for your product. A distributor who agrees to carry your product should also be seen as a partner. And if you communicate with and equip her as such, she will be more successful for you. Elevating any business relationship to a "partnership," even just in your attitude toward it, will usually bring better fortunes for all involved.

GETTING THE MOST OUT OF
YOUR HIRED AGENCIES

Even though you are the "client," the one paying for a service, your hired creative agencies should be regarded as partners. You share resources, goals, and the desire to get from the former to the latter most efficiently.

To help its employees and agencies work together, Microsoft periodically asks its advertising and PR firms to sit down and give a formal presentation explaining their guidelines for best results. This exercise effectively sets expectations about what Microsoft should anticipate from the ad agency and what the ad agency looks for from the client. The following three lessons come from an Anderson and Lembke agency presentation to Microsoft managers. These tips mostly show how to interact with an advertising team, but they could easily be applied to other agencies such as a PR firm, a promotions group, or a temporary sales force.

INFORMATIVE, INSPIRING INPUT TO GENERATE CREATIVE COMPELLING OUTPUT

A press release or promotion will only be as powerful as the information with which you arm your creative team. The right data on your product, competitive situation, and customer base can get your advertising agency, PR team, or promotions planner off to a flying start. Conversely, missing, vague, or incorrect data will ground them.

Microsoft managers submit "briefs" to their advertising agencies, promotion specialists, temporary sales forces, and public relations specialists to kick off a project. This exercise—finding the pertinent facts and presenting them in a straightforward, concise way—is great training for a marketer, whose job it is to communicate product benefits to a variety of audiences. Completeness, accuracy, and relevancy are prized. Hagiographies, superfluous technical details, and vague objectives are shunned. The following areas are critical to the creative brief:

- The problem or goal: Why are we doing this ad/PR/promotion?
- Marketing objective: What do we expect to get out of this? It helps if this is measurable. For example, "increase market share by 5 percent or sell X thousand units in next three months" will be easier to evaluate at the end of the project than "increase awareness of product."
- Product background: This includes when the product was introduced to the market, sales over the past few years, and any relevant competitive information. What does the product promise consumers? How is it differentiated from its competitors? What problem (if any) does it solve for people?
- Target audience: Toward whom is this product and this effort geared? What is the demographic, buying, or product-

satisfaction data on this group? There may be a primary and secondary audience. For example, teenage boys may be the primary audience for a computer game, but men in their twenties may also buy it. A tertiary audience, gift-givers, for example, may be considered too.

- Relevant marketing tactics: What other tactics are being used to market the product? How are competitors marketing their wares? What are the buying influences in this market (product reviews, word of mouth, in-store salespeople, etc.)?
- Budget/timing: How much can be spent and when should this thing happen? Should any selling seasons or expected competitor moves be taken into consideration?

The above points are usually backed up with data and examples to give the creative team a complete picture. Recent survey results from the target audience might be attached to the brief. Copies of competitors' ads may be sent over. Demonstrations of the product or competing products may be given. Telling the whole story with lots of props makes the situation come to life and gets the creative team more informed, more engaged, and more excited about their project.

INVOLVE THE AGENCY EARLY

Too often, a marketing team decides on their target audience, main messages, budget, and timing, months before calling in their advertising team. By the time they contact the agency, deadline pressures require the advertising team to create a big campaign in a short time. Of course, it's much harder to come up with something clever and compelling on short notice. But there are other reasons to give the agency more time and involvement in your plans.

THE AD AGENCY MAY BE ABLE TO CUSTOMIZE YOUR ADS TO A MAGAZINE'S ARTICLES

The Microsoft Encarta encyclopedia team gave their ad agency months to come up with a print campaign. After mulling the assignment over and coordinating the creative ideas with the media buyers, the agency decided to relate their ads to articles in a targeted magazine. They worked with the publisher to get the magazine's article schedule and created an ad campaign to match. In this case, *National Geographic* was publishing "Geo Guides." Each month Encarta ads featured a different tie-in to the magazine's subject matter, including the China Sea, volcanoes, etc.

Microsoft's agency suggested placing the ad across from the article. For example, they used the tag line "This might be the last page on the China Sea, but it's not the last word." They included a picture of the China Sea from inside Encarta and some information about the encyclopedia. The ad was almost an extension to the article. The advertising agency felt that people reading the article were more likely to look at the attached related information than to look at an ad that stood alone with a different subject matter.

It is expensive to create a new ad every month to match a magazine's stories, and most products aren't as versatile as an encyclopedia to customize to a magazine's content. But this is just one example of how involving an agency early can help you with your marketing plans. Without the time to think and plan, this successful campaign couldn't have happened.

THE AD AGENCY MAY USE THE ADVANCE NOTICE
TO RESERVE A SPECIAL SPOT IN THE MAGAZINE

To communicate how up-to-date Encarta's contents were, the advertising team also proposed linking an Encarta ad to the table of contents in magazines like *Newsweek*. The Encarta ad, with an arrow pointing to the table of contents, said, "Pick a story from the opposite page," and then encouraged readers to learn more with their kids on the subject, using Encarta. For the ad to make sense, it had to be across from the table of contents. In many magazines, that's a premium spot and needs to be reserved far in advance. Again, this creative idea wouldn't have come to fruition without a long planning period.

THEY MAY EVEN TELL YOU NOT TO DO AN AD

This one is somewhat unusual, but a good advertising team that's brought into the process early may tell you that an ad campaign isn't the best use of your marketing funds. The first priority for a packaged product is usually getting it on store shelves (all the ads in the world won't help you if a customer can't find your product) and then publicity (it's the cheapest way to get awareness). If these first two priorities aren't covered, don't advertise yet. For example, when a Microsoft team working on a new hardware product were told that fewer than expected stores had decided to carry the product, their advertising team agreed that it made sense to cancel a planned ad campaign.

Sometimes a long lead time isn't possible, especially if you are responding to a competitor's move or taking advantage of a surprise in the market. But if you have no excuse for doing things last minute, get your creative team going as soon as you have your objectives and budget nailed down.

THE AD TEAM SHOULD CREATE THE AD

Too often, the client team (you!) comes to a meeting with an ad already imagined. You might just say, "Hey, let's just show a beautiful photo of the product with the new price really big. People will know what the packaging looks like so they'll know what to look for in the store, and they'll know the price is great." Your idea may be valid. Then again, it may be rotten.

In any case, it doesn't give the ad agency—which you are paying for creative expertise—a fair shot. You are probably quite attached to your "great" idea and will measure anything they create against it. You've stymied their creative efforts before they have even begun, so you aren't going to get their best ideas. If you do have a specific idea in mind, you may as well tell them what it is before they do their brainstorming. They'll probably be able to incorporate your ideas into the final result, but will tweak it or twist it using their creative horsepower to make it more effective.

The marketing manager for one of Microsoft's CD-ROM titles told his ad agency team he wanted to do a print ad that would drive traffic to the stores clamoring for his product during the busy holiday season. The competitive situation was tight, with lots of high-quality rivals offering similar products. He thought a "letter to customers" explaining why Microsoft's product was better would be the perfect ad. He even went so far as to draft the letter and list the reasons.

The ad agency told the marketer that they felt a letter was more appropriate for PR emergencies, such as an airline strike or a food-tampering situation, and that in this case, most people would just pass over the ad in the newspaper. But the marketer still insisted he wanted a letter. The ad agency struggled with the marketer for days, trying to convince him that the letter was the wrong approach and to let them try some other implementations for the traffic-generating ad.

Finally, the ad team took the content of the marketing manager's idea—that Microsoft's CD had more information, top researchers, special product designers—and rolled it into an ad that used a great headline from a recent product review. This approach got the same message across but backed it up with quotes from objective, third-party reviewers. It gave more credibility to the message than a letter from Microsoft would have.

When the ad team showed their concept to the marketing manager, he loved it. The specific points he wanted to get across were there, and he had to agree that it sure beat his letter. The situation was successfully resolved, but the team lost precious days that they could have been using to brainstorm ideas.

If you have an idea for your ad, tell the agency. Let them think it over, throw it in the mix with their own ideas. But don't get so attached to your own inspiration that you can't see the merit of theirs. If you think you know more about creating stunning ads than your ad agency, you must have hired the wrong one (or you might be in the wrong job!). A strong ad team can let you know if your notion makes sense, why it's good or bad among other ideas, if you keep an open mind about it. The same holds true for public relations teams, promotions teams, and just about anyone else you hire for their creative talents and special expertise.

ONE AGENCY DOESN'T FIT ALL

Microsoft pitches its products to a variety of audiences—from geeky software programmers to managers of corporate information systems to neophyte home PC buyers. They've chosen different PR agencies to design messages and programs for each group, depending on the agency's expertise. "I used to think if a PR agency could communicate to one target, all they had to do was learn about another target and they could communicate to that one too," says Janet Angell, group marketing manager of the Microsoft Network. "But having Microsoft's technical PR firm talk to brand-new computer users was like asking a pastry chef to make sushi."

A good PR firm helps reporters and writers get smart on a subject. Waggener Edstrom, Microsoft's PR agency for many years, devoted itself to PC trade publications and to mainstream writers who covered the PC industry. When Microsoft started making CD-ROMs and other software for the home PC user, Waggener Edstrom was at somewhat of a loss. They didn't know how to package a story to get on *Oprah* or in *Sports Illustrated* and *Cosmopolitan*. They didn't have the contacts to call or the right pitch to make on a software product. The fifty-page technical reviewer's guide they always handed out just wasn't appropriate for a *USA Today* writer. Waggener Edstrom did a great job in their area of expertise, but that expertise didn't extend into the vast world of *Good Morning America, Working Mother,* and *Modern Maturity.* (Since then, they have shored up this area and created their own New Media group.)

Instead of forcing the square peg of Waggener to fit into the round hole of consumer press coverage, Microsoft hired a round peg, Edelman Public Relations Worldwide, which specialized in reaching media folks who might not understand technology themselves, let alone be able to discuss it with their audience. Instead of sending out thick technical reviewer's guides, Edelman called to pitch stories like "Top Ten Holiday Gifts...Give Someone an E-mail Account" to boost awareness of Microsoft's free E-mail service, MSN HotMail. They would package a story that was focused on the product benefit, rather than pitching a story about the product itself.

Edelman would create tips for consumers that promoted Microsoft software. So, coinciding with Labor Day, for example, they pitched a story called "Using the Internet to Get a Job." The story advised sending your résumé to prospective employers using HotMail E-mail and checking for messages from recruiters from anywhere in the world using HotMail, along with other tips such as "go to company Web sites to research companies that interest you" and "see on-line city guides to get the flavor of a new town." These kinds of ideas generated terrific coverage in the mainstream media.

When you're hiring a PR firm, ask them to be frank about their capabilities. Ask to see samples of their work and the results they have achieved. Review their lists of media contacts for your trade publications or whatever media you want to focus on. Make sure they know your constituency and what those customers watch, read, and care about. In Microsoft's case, the company needed both the technical and industry experience of Waggener Edstrom, coupled with an agency whose expertise lay in the popular press.

THE RIGHT-FLAVORED CARROT ALONG WITH THE PROPERLY SHARPENED STICK

The carrot or the stick. Either on its own might garner the results you want in your business dealings. However, combining them and then fine-tuning them to the parties you are dealing with will magnify their effects.

As the OEM (original equipment manufacturer) Global Marketing Initiatives manager in 1996, Samir Bodas wanted to "go where no other Microsoftie had gone before." That is, into the emerging markets of Brazil, India, China, Russia, and Indonesia. The growth of PC sales in those countries was fabulous. According to his estimates, China purchased 2 million personal computers in 1996 and was on track to buy 5 million in the year 1999. These were significant numbers. Five million PCs was the yearly volume a large European country would buy. The dilemma was that the number of copies of Microsoft Windows sold was a small fraction of the total PC base, even though almost every PC shipped with a copy of Windows on it. The young manager had run smack into the hotbed of software piracy.

Software piracy in these countries was emerging as quickly as the PC markets. No public stigma was attached to pirating sortware. The value of intellectual property rights was not understood. Illegal software copying was becoming a favorite of organized-crime families in China, Russia, and other countries. These criminals found that the ratio of profit to risk was more enticing in the software market than in other illegal activities such as dealing drugs. To enter the piracy business, they didn't need a poppy field. They didn't need a drug processing plant or a network of couriers. They didn't have to worry about the U.S. Drug Enforcement Agency swooping down on them. And the margins were wonderful.

Rather than fighting with organized crime lords, Samir, working with the local Microsoft teams, took a three-pronged approach to three keenly interested groups in those countries: the government, the sellers of the PCs, and the end customers. Each group had different needs and motivations for making the software market more legitimate in their country.

At the government level, Microsoft (and others, of course) had to convince the country's leaders that they needed to respect and protect intellectual property. The unauthorized production of copyrighted software, pharmaceuticals, music, and videos disregarded this. Microsoft knew these countries wanted to be leaders among the developing economies and among their neighbors. The countries wanted to be seen as legitimate and safe places to do business in order to attract foreign investments. Microsoft argued that protecting intellectual property rights and cracking down on piracy was key to this legitimacy.

There was also the tax loss. When a government realized the money it was losing by not collecting taxes on the pirated materials, it was more eager to legitimize those businesses.

Microsoft and other companies also demonstrated that piracy squelched the local development of those industries (software, pharmaceuticals, music, and video) because there was no incentive to invent when the invention wasn't protected. Pointing to the U.S. software market and its key place in the growth of the U.S. economy of the 1980s, Microsoft made a strong statement for the importance of developing that industry and the others. These industries could help drive the whole country's economy up.

Microsoft took another approach with the large computer makers—the folks who were buying the pirated software and selling it on their PCs. Samir and the Microsoft team learned that a major goal of these computer makers was to expand their sales to include overseas customers and to international businesses that had set up local branches in their country.

Microsoft wanted to convince the PC makers that buying their Windows software legitimately was the key to increasing sales and expanding their markets in other countries. Firms abroad and local international firms were wary of buying any computer systems with illegal software. They did not want to run afoul of any local or international laws. Microsoft offered ways to help the PC makers gain the legitimacy and respect they needed to be players in the global supply of personal computers. Here, both the carrot and the stick were useful.

A variety of incentives and rewards were offered. PC makers who bought legal copies of Windows and subjected themselves to inspections and other authorization procedures could become a Microsoft "partner." As a partner, they could do joint press releases with Microsoft, letting potential customers know that the PC maker was a viable business partner. Microsoft managers would accompany them on major sales calls as evidence of their legitimacy and ties to the company. And, the PC maker's executives had access to top Microsoft executives to voice their opinions regarding the future of the software.

Those who sold pirated software were prosecuted under local laws. This both punished the lawbreakers and showed the legitimate "partner" companies another way in which Microsoft was helping them to succeed, i.e., by ridding them of their unfair competition.

The last group were the mom-and-pop PC builders. They weren't big enough to go after international sales, so legitimacy and respect didn't matter as much to them, but they wanted to expand their business locally. They used pirated software as a competitive cost advantage against legitimate suppliers. Samir tried to make the move to legitimacy attractive for these companies who would "get genuine."

Companies who "got genuine" were listed in local Microsoft ads—marketing funds were spent on their behalf. Microsoft technical staff became available to help them with their Windows software installation problems and questions. Some of the top company executives were flown to Seattle for a presentation by Bill Gates and other executives on the future of the PC and PC software. At trade shows, training sessions, and conferences, the Microsoft "genuine" companies received special badges, stood in shorter registration lines, and were invited to dinners with Microsoft executives.

Microsoft also involved customers in the get-genuine campaign. For example, in India, they ran a lottery for customers, who, by entering their official Microsoft product license number, could win a car. This raised the awareness of pirated versus nonpirated software among customers and encouraged them to ask for legitimacy from their computer dealer.

The three months of the get-genuine campaign in India increased sales of Windows to PC makers by 3,000 percent (yes, it's three thousand percent—that's not a typo). Once PC makers became used to being a Microsoft partner, they saw the value of staying legitimate via good-quality software, marketing funds, free training, and joint advertising. The specter of increased legal action against pirates always accompanied these incentives.

Samir and the anti-piracy group examined the goals and desires of every party to the piracy equation and designed their plans accordingly. Industry growth and tax revenue for governments, international legitimacy for large companies, and marketing funds for smaller companies were tailored to each group's needs. Optimizing for each part helped the effort as a whole.

IN A NEW JOB, START WITH WHAT YOU ALREADY KNOW

Arriving at a new company or switching jobs internally can be overwhelming. Who's who? What needs to get done and what's the best way to go about doing it? After you've figured out your responsibilities, reviewed your priorities, and met your coworkers, sometimes the best thing to start with is the area you already know.

Succeeding in your first task will likely boost your overall performance and give new coworkers clear evidence of your abilities. Don't always tackle the prickliest problem right off. What's the most familiar thing on your to-do list? Do that assignment first (as long as it is somewhat substantial). If possible, let the learning curve wait a little until you can make a good impression.

When twenty-eight-year-old Jeff Camp transferred to Tokyo as business manager for Microsoft's Far East region, no one knew what to expect from him. The difficult tasks he faced ranged from streamlining inefficient order-taking to negotiating possible joint ventures. To make matters even more difficult, he was only an "internal consultant." He did not control the businesses he was analyzing. He did not own the budgets. The teams did not report to him. He was just there to present his opinions and try to convince those around him to act on those opinions. His success would be determined by his ability to influence managers in the region—none of whom knew him at all. That his predecessor was seen by some as an arrogant nose-in-others'-business guy only made his task that much worse.

When he arrived in Tokyo, Jeff looked through his list of potential projects for something with which he was familiar. He wanted to make an impact on the business and start off on the right foot with his new colleagues. As a product manager for Windows 95 in the United States, Jeff had worked with creators of computer games. He knew from his former job that software makers in Japan—home to Sony PlayStation, Nintendo, and Sega—produced most of the best-selling games in the world. At the same time, none of the top games for Windows were made in Japan. Microsoft's support of Japanese game companies bordered between negligent and nonexistent. This problem was not on Jeff's list, but Windows 95 was approaching release in Japan, and he knew it was an area that needed help. He also knew he had the right experience to fix the situation. His boss gave him the go-ahead to give it a try.

Capitalizing on the knowledge from his Windows 95 job, Jeff set about creating world-class technical support for Japanese game-makers interested in programming for Windows 95. He persuaded the technical group in the United States to translate the Software Development Kit, showing how different features of Windows 95 could be used to make a game. He held the first Windows games developer conference in Japan, allowing big companies and small to learn the new technology, meet each other, get Windows 95 training, and brainstorm problems with technical folks from Microsoft. When Windows 95 launched in Japan, games became some of the best-selling software products on the platform.

By using his previous experience to add value to his new group, Jeff gained credibility. Later, when he tackled other issues, he found he had the confidence of his colleagues, who had watched him identify a need, come up with ideas for its solution, and successfully implement resulting plans.

About a year later, Jeff was discussing a business opportunity with Makoto Naruke, president of Microsoft Japan and Masayoshi Son, the chairman of Japan's largest software distributor, who is sometimes called the "Bill Gates of Japan." Discussing possible acquisitions in Japanese, Jeff meant to say to Masayoshi Son, "Sometimes I think you really like buy-outs." Unfortunately, he used the word *baishun* rather than the proper term *baishu* and ended up saying, "Sometimes I think you really like prostitution." The room went silent.

Jeff's boss leaned over and asked in English, "Did you mean *acquisitions*?"

Jeff said, "Yes. What did I say?"

As Makoto Naruke explained the mistake, Jeff turned beet red, smiling and apologizing profusely. While he attributes getting off the hook to a positive attitude and a smile—"a good heart can overcome a bad vocabulary"—Jeff's earlier good work had earned him a solid reputation and allowed him this gaffe.

Three Lessons I've Learned about Making My Customer a Partner

Kristin Weeber, Reseller Account Executive,
working with Dell Computer:

1. **Identify the key contacts inside the account before your first visit.**
   Who are the decision-makers? Does your product line have advocates or skeptics in the account? Don't waste three months just trying to figure out whom to talk to.
2. **Learn the account's expectations of their account manager before you start.**
   How often do you need to be there? How quickly do their questions need to get answered? Do they want you to be a partner or an order taker?
3. **Find out anything you can about the company's corporate culture.**
   Learn their protocols for decision-making and work flow. Find out what they value. Understanding and adapting to the culture at your account helps you to be perceived as part of the team, and ultimately, it increases productivity and reduces frustration when you're driving projects to completion.

ABSENT PARTNERS: BE NICE, EVEN WHEN THEY'RE NOT IN THE ROOM

Murphy's Law would state that when you tell your boss that the intern down the hall is a dimwit, that the intern down the hall will turn out to be the boss's niece. The clever E-mail you wrote making your coworker the butt of a joke inevitably makes its way to the butt's in-box. So take your mom's advice. No, not the one about clean underwear and the emergency room. Play nicely with the other kids or they won't want to play with you.

A Microsoft programmer walked into a meeting where each of five software teams were going to talk about new capabilities they were going to add to their products. He looked around the table and didn't see anyone from the PowerPoint product team. Rolling his eyes, he said, "Great, those PowerPoint bozos aren't here. They probably want to add some sparkly stars or dancing balls to their product." As he was saying this, the people in the room gestured wildly at a speakerphone sitting in the middle of the table. The programmer, now realizing the PowerPoint team was on conference call, could do nothing but wind up his sentence lamely, "Oh. Hi, Brendan." For years after, whenever the programmer would walk into a meeting, someone would say, "Hey, PowerPoint's on the phone," whether they were or not.

You will be tempted to make a sarcastic remark about the coworker who is not up to snuff. You will want to describe, *in excruciating detail,* how the other guy tripped up your good results with his ineptitude. You'd like to tell your office-mate that your friendship is the result of propinquity, not his or her indescribable disposition. In general, it's good policy to let off this kind of steam with someone who is certain not to repeat it—like your newborn baby or your deaf great-aunt—rather than get yourself in trouble.

Ten Things I've Wanted to Say in the Office but Didn't

Author Unknown

1. I don't know what your problem is, but I'll bet it's hard to pronounce.
2. It's a thankless job, but I've got a lot of Karma to burn off.
3. How about never? Is never good for you?
4. The fact that no one understands you doesn't mean you're an artist.
5. Yes, I am an agent of Satan, but my duties are largely ceremonial.
6. You sound reasonable.... Time to up my medication.
7. I'll try being nicer if you'll try being smarter.
8. Who, me? I just wander from room to room.
9. I see you've set aside this special time to humiliate yourself in public.
10. Someday we'll look back on this, laugh nervously, and change the subject.

THINK YOU'VE REALLY
SCREWED UP?

Blown something big? Maybe it's not as bad as you think. And even if it is pretty horrendous, getting in front of the damage by apologizing, fixing, or quickly showing it won't happen again will minimize your personal fallout.

A friend called me up one day and said, "I just blew it! I had prepared a presentation for my division vice president to give to some potential partners about our new products, and when we all walked in for the meeting, she asked me to do the talking. Well, of course, I hadn't prepared to give the speech, was incredibly nervous in front of her, and felt tongue-tied, flustered, and stupid during the entire thing. I don't have too many interactions with her since she's higher in the food chain, and now I'm sure she thinks I'm a moron." Since the presentation was made to upper-level executives from Fortune 500 companies who had flown in *just* to hear about Microsoft's new product offerings, he had reason to be worried.

Have you ever been caught off guard and felt that you didn't handle the situation well? Usually these things seem drastically worse to the person they are happening to than to the other folks in the room. In my friend's case, chances are he did fine. But if he was really concerned about his performance, he could have sent the VP an E-mail or stopped by her office and said simply, "I wasn't at my best today. I didn't know I'd be doing the presentation, so I didn't prepare. From now on, I'll plan to talk through the slides I create and will do a much better job."

Getting the perceived screwup out in the open gives the manager the chance to say, "Don't worry, it was fine." Or, if you really did screw up, she knows you're aware of it and are striving to improve. In any case, your boss will see you as someone who wants to do high-quality work and is willing to toil to get results. It sure is better than stewing in your office, imagining the horrid things she's thinking about you!

Three Lessons I've Learned about Working with an Executive

From a former business-strategy analyst working for Steve Ballmer (Microsoft's current president):

1. **Understand the executive's language.**
   When I worked for Steve Ballmer, he thought and spoke at the speed of light, often talking in shorthand. If your boss speaks in acronyms, metaphors, or jargon, make sure you know what he or she is saying before you leave the room. Don't try to figure it out later alone at your desk. Don't be afraid to confirm what you think you heard. It's better than coming back later with the wrong information.

2. **Learn the executive's hot buttons.**
   Pushing someone's "hot button" gets him or her very worried or excited. Know what's going to ignite the passions of the person you are talking to. Whenever you present an idea, results, or status, address his or her top three concerns up front since you know those are key issues.

3. **When possible, get corroboration on your data or opinion from someone your boss trusts.**
   I once told Steve we needed a whole list of sales tools for the sales force. "No, we don't," he said. I told him I had gotten this prioritized list from the ten most senior field marketing guys and named them. After that, he agreed.

MANAGING THROUGH PEOPLE'S FILTERS

You've heard the adage "people hear what they want to hear." This is often, unfortunately, true up and down the management chain. You've seen employees who ignore constructive criticism but lap up compliments. Maybe you've had a manager who cared only about his pet projects and zoned out when you talked about problems where you needed help. Recognize and plan for these filters in advance to get your desired outcome.

Kathleen Schoenfelder had a great idea for her software, Microsoft Project. The new feature would help manage and coordinate multiple projects in a department. Knowing her boss's hot buttons, she did not just go in and say, "This will really help users. Can I have four extra programmers to make it happen?" Instead, Kathleen told her boss, "I can contribute to the tracking component of knowledge management." Next, she went to the boss of her boss, for the next level of approval. To him, she said, "This will work with our Office and Back Office products to help people automate their work processes. It'll help make us a key technical partner in how they run their business." Both agreed, each based on the reason she gave them.

Kathleen's boss was part of a division-wide mission to define and create solutions for "knowledge management," a new buzz word that described white-collar workers—those people who worked in a "sea of knowledge." Components of knowledge management included document creation, editing, routing, accessing information and tagging it, and tracking assignments. By plugging into one of these areas, an area where her boss was being held accountable, Kathleen's proposal seemed a lot more attractive.

One level up, her boss's boss was responsible for all of Microsoft's business software working together. Because Kathleen's idea made Project work with Office and Back Office, her request would help his area of focus as well.

To Kathleen, the idea was appealing because it would help customers, increase satisfaction ratings, maybe help win reviews, and boost sales. But the idea had other merits as well, merits that mattered to her management chain. Focusing on what they cared about helped her idea take hold. Kathleen's bosses were responsible for billions of dollars in Microsoft revenues. Her idea not only helped her own piece of the business, but the larger pie as well, which helped sell her bosses on it.

Filters can sometimes work against you if you don't know about them. In the mid-1990s, Microsofties knew of an unpleasant perception in the business world. Meeting with Microsoft as a potential partner was seen as risky because, instead of forming a partnership, Microsoft might do the business venture on its own, using the information you gave it in the meeting. To allay this fear, Microsoft managers would go into meetings saying, "I need to tell you we plan on making a big play in this category with or without you." The Microsoft folks figured they were being candid about the possibility that they might embark on the venture alone. They figured this news would keep the potential partner from divulging proprietary or secret information to them during the meeting.

The Microsoft managers failed to realize one thing. There was the feeling—some call it paranoia—in the business world that Microsoft wanted to take over not only every software category, but also every other business in the world. This included banking, real estate, classified advertising, and any other lucrative business it could find. Instead of hearing an admonition from the Microsoft managers to refrain from divulging information, these potential partners only heard a threat. To them, when the person from Microsoft said, "I need to tell you we plan on making a big play in this category with or without you," what they heard was, "Play with us or we'll go it alone and beat you!" It wasn't the case—*really!*

Some filters are just politeness. When a senior executive asks the person presenting to a roomful of thirty people, "Do you think we could be more aggressive in this area?" She is usually saying, "*I* think we *should* be more aggressive in this area," in a way that doesn't make the presenter feel so defensive. Recognize these filtered statements. Listen for the message under the tact.

Three Lessons I've Learned about Meetings

Eva Corets, Group Advertising Manager,
Interactive Media Group:

1. **Synthesize your thoughts.**
   Don't give the unabridged chapter and verse unless asked because no one has time for *all* of the details.
2. **Know who the real decision-maker is.**
   Someone may claim to have the power, but often people above can overrule that decision. Are they in the meeting? They need to be.
3. **Spend more time listening than talking.**
   You'll be surprised how much you learn.

STARTING WITH A
GRACEFUL EXIT

When you're going into a marriage, the last thing you want to talk about is what would happen if someone wanted a divorce. It's the same with business partnerships. The parties are usually so eager to work together that they neglect an "exit clause" in their contract. They may be foaming over a wonderful opportunity that's coupled with an impending deadline and can't imagine any reason things won't go as planned. Or they may not want to ask, "What if one of us wants to back out, or something goes wrong?" for fear of spooking their potential partner, who may then get the idea that they are not committed to the venture.

But getting clarity on the why, when, and who owns what in case the alliance doesn't work out will save you time, bad feelings, and possibly a lawsuit. In its Consumer Division, Microsoft made this mistake a few times before changing the way they wrote contracts. The teams were focused on the CD-ROM software they were building and how to enhance the next generation of products. When the Internet hit them full force and eviscerated the CD-ROM market, the need for a termination clause became apparent. By then, other contracts had been written without one.

In the early 1990s Microsoft licensed materials from a variety of companies to build CD-ROMs for home PCs. The materials were text, pictures, sounds, and video that the Microsoft development team wove together with interesting links to create CD-ROMs on everything from gardening to dog care. Most of the material suppliers wanted to join forces with Microsoft to get a jump on the nascent CD-ROM market. They could provide the words, pictures, and videos. Then, Microsoft would market and, more importantly, distribute the CD-ROMs. Microsoft had a large, established presence in software stores.

This made it easier for them to obtain shelf space for new products than their partners, even those with big names, such as *Reader's Digest* and Julia Child.

Because they were partnering with Microsoft, most of the companies providing the CD-ROM content didn't build their own CD-ROMs at the same time. They were relying on Microsoft for a way to enter, learn about, and make money in the market. Unfortunately for both parties, a robust content-based CD-ROM market never materialized. No one could do anything about it. The Internet was growing and soon obliterated the CD-ROM market.

Microsoft had invested millions of dollars in these CD-ROMs, but saw there was little point in marketing them aggressively (i.e., expensively). Retailers didn't want the products taking up valuable shelf space if they wouldn't sell well. Microsoft shifted focus to the Internet and began cutting the CD-ROM projects.

Enter the problem of no exit clause. The content-company partners felt Microsoft was abandoning them. These partners had held off on developing their own products independently because Microsoft was going to do it with them. Now Microsoft looked to be dropping the ball. One partner threatened to sue Microsoft for not distributing and marketing their products as promised.

Both sides had valid positions. And both sides would have been better off if they had had the forethought to put "exit language" in the contract. Exit language includes

- Valid reasons to terminate the contract
- Penalties for terminating the contract for a reason not listed
- Period of notification one party has to give the other to terminate
- Who owes what money to whom, based on the termination
- Who owns the rights to the intellectual property or product in case of termination

There might still be hard feelings, and it's hard to think of all the reasons why you might need to terminate, but the list above will help extricate you from a sticky situation and reduce your chances of getting sued.

In other cases, the vagaries of the contract's exit language allowed content companies to compete with Microsoft as soon as Microsoft stopped helping them. As part of the contract to get content for some CD-ROMs or games, Microsoft would hire the content owners to help create the CD itself. The people in the content company were happy to do this because they wanted to learn how to build software, and Microsoft was going to teach them. Using Microsoft technology and Microsoft employees to train them, they soon knew how to build CD-ROMs and games.

Once they learned how to create CD-ROMs, a few partner companies decided to make them entirely on their own, competing directly with Microsoft. No language in the termination clause stated who owned what and what could be done with the content and technology. Microsoft was in essence creating and training competition. The Microsoft lawyers just shook their heads in resignation when they saw ex-partners hitting the stores with new and successful products. Again, both sides had valid concerns and courses of action, but both would have had an easier, clearer path if the contract had been more specific.

Three Things I Learned about Finding a Good Partner

CJ Liu Rosenblatt, Business Development Manager, Interactive Media Division:

1. **Work with the decision-maker.**

   If your contact has to go get approval three levels up every time he talks to you, ask to work directly with the person who is actually making the decisions. If you're still stuck working with a junior employee after that, your partner must not value the deal very highly.

2. **Make sure your partner knows the value you are bringing to the deal, or you won't get the best price for it.**

   We showed our CarPoint Web site to a car seller who basically said, "Um, that's nice." She didn't realize how hard it was to create the software, how popular it was with customers, or how much money she could make from it. Our job was to demonstrate those things. In contrast, a leading brokerage company had seen our Investor "portfolio manager" on the Web and had tried to create one of their own. Two years later they asked to buy our portfolio manager because they realized they couldn't make a high-quality one themselves—by then they were willing to pay big bucks.

3. **Cultural fit is key.**

   You don't have to manage everything exactly the same as your partner, but you should have the same mind-set on key practices. We've worked with discount brokerage firms used to a fast-paced, constantly changing environment, so they're willing to try new things, make decisions quickly, the same as we are. We've also worked with financial institutions whose whole goal was to minimize risk and limit change. That was a bit more challenging, to say the least.

IF SOMETHING'S EATING UP YOUR TIME, MAKE SURE YOUR BOSS AGREES ON THE MENU

You may be doing the world's best work... but on the wrong project. Agree with your boss on how to prioritize your work and let him or her know if those priorities change. Don't waste your Herculean efforts. Partner with your boss to agree on your to-do list.

Microsoft Sidewalk is an on-line service in major cities that lists entertainment venues and movie times, reviews restaurants, and generally helps you plan your free time and social life. In 1996, Microsoft plunked $100 million into this service, making it one of the company's biggest investments for the future.

With three months to go before the launch, publicity "crises" kept popping up. Ticketmaster was suing Sidewalk for linking into the middle of their Web site, bypassing Ticketmaster's home page (and more importantly, their ads). Reporters were calling to get Microsoft's side of the story. On another front, local newspapers felt that by producing its own city guide, Microsoft was taking away newspaper advertising revenues, and lots of reporters were calling to learn about Microsoft's plans. Yet another reporter got word on a possible joint venture and was calling to sniff it out.

A new employee at Microsoft was working with Sidewalk's PR team, and she regularly stepped in to deflect the PR crisis that sometimes made Sidewalk the priority of the day. Due to this hard work and team effort, the reporters got the information they wanted and the fires were calmed. The Sidewalk crises were averted and plans moved forward. So when the end of the year came, she was disappointed that her efforts actually contributed to a negative review. Her boss informed her that she had placed too much importance on the Sidewalk project, which was not listed as a key objective in her review goals.

The new review period was starting and she didn't want to run into the same situation. It would have been nice if her boss had been more involved in general, asking her about the status of various things and guiding her priorities along the way. Because her boss wasn't a hands-on manager, it was up to her to do the communicating.

She made a list of her major objectives and projects for the upcoming months. She ranked them by importance. She showed the list to her boss and got feedback on her priorities. She made sure they agreed on what was critical and how success would be defined. Every few months, she went back with the priority list and updated her boss on her progress. Were there things that should be added, removed, or reranked? Clearly communicating with her boss and mapping to her objectives became a priority so there sould be no surprises in the upcoming review period.

If your boss doesn't know what you're working on, or you have shifted your priorities without clearly communicating your change in course to your boss, you could be spinning your wheels in the wrong direction. Make sure he or she agrees with your plans before you expend any effort.

LET YOUR BOSS SAY NO
(TO OTHER PEOPLE)

Feeling overwhelmed? Are your coworkers asking you to do too much? Are you carrying the whole team? Let your boss be your gatekeeper. Ask her to say no for you. Enlist her to lighten your workload by telling people you're unavailable. You'll keep your can-do reputation. You won't disappoint people. And you'll finally be able to get your own work done.

A very gentle marketer worked on CD-ROM products for the home including a CD on Frank Lloyd Wright, one on dogs, and another on pilots and flying machines. He really liked the people he worked with. He helped them when they were on tight deadlines or facing big workloads. He pitched in when they were having a hard day and was happy to do so. One would say, "Would you review this memo for me?" Another would ask him to dig up some old sales figures or send some CDs to a charity for its annual auction. He never wanted to let his coworkers down. He was a great help, but, unfortunately, he didn't have enough time to do his own job well. He worked longer hours but still turned in a less-than-stellar performance.

He went to his boss to let her know what was happening since she had remarked on his performance—or lack thereof. Together they figured out a way to refocus him on his duties. More importantly, if his coworkers asked for help, the marketer would tell them he'd like to help, but his boss had him working on a bunch of things. He'd say, "If you want, you can go to her to request my help." This dissuaded most folks. For those that persisted, he let his boss be the heavy. When she said he was unavailable, he didn't take the blame from coworkers who were asking him to do things. And happily, he could stop eating dinner at his desk.

KEEP THE PRICING SIMPLE
SO YOUR DISTRIBUTORS CAN
CONCENTRATE ON
SELLING THE PRODUCT

Economic theory tells us the demand curve slopes. By picking a single pricing point, you automatically lose money because some folks would pay more for your product than the price you picked. Using this theory, some managers set a variety of prices for their products. A businessperson and a tourist on the same flight have probably paid vastly different sums for their tickets. A bottle of wine in the supermarket costs more than a restaurant might pay for that same wine. However, if your pricing gets so complicated it gets in the way of sales, you won't get the extra revenue. Simplifying the process may generate better returns.

The "Upgrade Your World" promotion was a Microsoft pricing fiasco. At first, it seemed like a great way to boost sales of products that go with Microsoft Office and get people to try some of the fun CD-ROM products that weren't selling too well. However, imagine store clerks—many of them temporary—in the Christmas shopping season trying to explain the promotion. "Buy a copy of Microsoft Office and one other product from this list (show list of ten products) and get a CD-ROM free (show them the other list). Now, if you already own Microsoft Office, the rules change a bit. Buy Microsoft Office for $229 plus...blah...blah... blah."

The outcome? No one at Microsoft seemed to be able to explain this promotion. No one at the retail level seemed prepared to implement it. Holiday shoppers in a rush were frustrated by it. The objective made sense at the start, but the complexity of the sales program killed it.

Too many variations of the same product can also generate
costly confusion. In 1993 Microsoft introduced a new version
of Windows, the first to include networking capabilities such as
sharing printers and sending E-mail. There were different types
of customers who might use the new product, so Microsoft created seven different versions of it. There were separate products for Microsoft DOS users, Windows 3.1 users, and
brand-new-computer users. There was also a starter kit that
included networking cards and cables for two computers, and
an add-on kit to hook up additional computers.

It was hard to explain the difference between the products,
so customers weren't sure which to buy. It was expensive to
stock seven products on their shelves, so software sellers chose
just two or three. Sales were anemic. Microsoft got the message
and reduced the variations down to two for their next version,
eliminating customer bewilderment and lowering inventory
carrying costs.

Three Lessons I've Learned about Working with Partners on the Road

Jeff Raikes, Group Vice President:

I spend lots of time on the road, once logging twenty-six thousand miles in two consecutive weeks. The way I get the most out of each trip is to

1. **Hear what's really going on from the front-line managers.** Find out the three most important issues they're facing.
2. **Teach employees by example.**
   The way an executive explains the company strategy, answers thorny questions, or presents a new product line can be a great teaching tool, just by demonstration.
3. **Write up a trip report.**
   (After the trip mentioned above, Jeff cranked out a forty-two-page report of to-dos, new resource requirements, and a summary of the key themes that he believed should drive the next steps in Microsoft strategy. That report informed and guided his team and provided feedback to the groups he visited.)

Epilogue

Somebody once said that there's no such thing as a career ladder. It's really more like a spiral staircase. The same is true for your business. Don't expect a direct steady climb. You'll need to make some forays to the side as you experiment with new ideas. You may feel like you're going in circles, not making any progress, only to look back and see how far you've come. And like a spiral staircase, it may take a lot longer to reach the top than it would appear to when you start.

Managers are often unsure about making decisions and manipulating the critical factors that determine the success of their business. When these questions and factors become numerous, the market is changing and competitor moves seem unknowable, any additional problem can leave you flummoxed. The purpose of this book was to take you behind-the-scenes at one of the world's most successful businesses to introduce you to the practices and processes of leaders there. I hope that delving into a new framework or learning about different approaches to common situations has given you more tools to use when your business faces those circumstances. Break down the daunting problem or question into its smallest pieces and solve those parts one by one. Use the examples in this book to spin off your own ideas and new ways to do things.

Don't worry about making mistakes—everyone does it, even the United States Department of Justice. Amongst the millions of internal corporate E-mails they were sifting through, some DOJ lawyers found and submitted for evidence the fact that a very senior Microsoft vice president said that the "Windows Paradise" was under threat and the "Netscape pollution must be eradicated." Damning evidence in their antitrust case? No, it turned out that the head of the sales force was parodying hip-hop star Coolio's "Gangsta's Paradise," a popular rap song, for the amusement of his team.

Fabulous luck and some competitor mis-steps have paved Microsoft's road to success but unless the principles described in this book had been at work, the road ahead would've lead to nowhere. The lessons and ideas in my first book, *All I Really Need to Know in Business I Learned at Microsoft,* show how Microsofties excel in their jobs as managers and guide their careers. This book took the advice of some of the company's highest-ranking leaders to show how to win in business and on the Web. Combine the two, and I believe your company will prosper, your career will thrive, and you'll have fun with both!